# What People Are Saying about Threshold Bible Study

"Besides furnishing the reader with solid biblical analysis, this remarkable series provides a method of study and reflection, for both individuals and groups, that is bound to produce rich fruit. This well-developed thematic approach to Bible study is meant to wed serious study and personal prayer within a reflective context. Stephen Binz is to be applauded for this fine addition to Bible study programs."

Dianne Bergant, CSA, professor of Old Testament,
Catholic Theological Union, Chicago

"The Threshold Bible Study connects the wisdom of God's Word to our daily lives. This fine series will provide needed tools that can deepen your understanding of Scripture, but most importantly it can deepen your faith. In the classical tradition of *lectio divina*, this series also offers a very practical way to pray with Scripture, and I can think of nothing better for equipping people for the New Evangelization than a biblically soaked life of prayer." Most Reverend Charles J. Chaput, OFM Cap., Archbishop of Denver

"In an increasingly Bible-reading and Bible-praying Church these helpful books combine solid biblical information and challenging suggestions for personal and group prayer. By covering a wide variety of themes and topics they continually breathe new life into ancient texts." John R. Donahue, SJ, Raymond E. Brown Professor Emeritus of New Testament Studies, St. Mary's Seminary and University, Baltimore

"Threshold Bible Study successfully bridges the painful gap between solid biblical scholarship and the rich spiritual nourishment that we expect to find in the words of Scripture. In this way, indispensable biblical knowledge leads to that spiritual wisdom which enables us to live in accord with God's purposes. Stephen Binz is to be congratulated for responding to this urgent need in today's world." Demetrius Dumm, OSB, Professor of New Testament, Saint Vincent Seminary, Saint Vincent Archabbey, Latrobe, Pennsylvania

"Threshold Bible Study offers a marvelous new approach for individuals and groups to study themes in our rich biblical and theological tradition. Moving through these thematic units feels like gazing at panels of stained glass windows, viewing similar images through different lights." John Endres, SJ, professor of Scripture, Jesuit School of Theology, Berkeley

"Threshold Bible Study provi~~ ~~lical themes, enabling Catholics to read, with greater ~~ ~~. When studied along with the documents of Vatica~ ~~ ~~*Church*, this series can be a help for personal and gro~~ ~~rdinal George, OMI, ~~ ~~:chbishop of Chicago

D1530214

"The distance many feel between the Word of God and their everyday lives can be overwhelming. It need not be so. Threshold Bible Study is a fine blend of the best of biblical scholarship and a realistic sensitivity to the spiritual journey of the believing Christian. I recommend it highly."     Francis J. Moloney, SDB, biblical scholar, educator, author, and Provincial Superior of the Salesians of Don Bosco in Australia

"Stephen Binz offers an invaluable guide that can make reading the Bible enjoyable (again) and truly nourishing. A real education on how to read the Bible, this series prepares people to discuss Scripture and to share it in community."     Jacques Nieuviarts, professor of Scripture, Institut Catholique de Toulouse, France

"Threshold Bible Study is appropriately named, for its commentary and study questions bring people to the threshold of the text and invite them in. The questions guide but do not dominate. They lead readers to ponder and wrestle with the biblical passages and take them across the threshold toward life with God. Stephen Binz's work stands in the tradition of the biblical renewal movement and brings it back to life. We need more of this in the Church."     Kathleen M. O'Connor, Professor of Old Testament, Columbia Theological Seminary

"Threshold Bible Study is an enriching and enlightening approach to understanding the rich faith which the Scriptures hold for us today. Written in a clear and concise style, Threshold Bible Study presents solid contemporary biblical scholarship, offers questions for reflection and/or discussion, and then demonstrates a way to pray from the Scriptures. All these elements work together to offer the reader a wonderful insight into how the sacred texts of our faith can touch our lives in a profound and practical way today. I heartily recommend this series to both individuals and to Bible study groups."
Abbot Gregory J. Polan, OSB, Conception Abbey and Seminary College

"Threshold Bible Study helpfully introduces the lay reader into the life-enhancing process of lectio divina or prayerful reading of Scripture, individually or in a group. This series, prepared by a reputable biblical scholar and teacher, responds creatively to the exhortation of the Council to provide God's people abundant nourishment from the table of God's Word. The process proposed leads the reader from Bible study to personal prayer, community involvement, and active Christian commitment in the world."
Sandra M. Schneiders,
Professor of New Testament and Spirituality,
Jesuit School of Theology, Berkeley

"Threshold Bible Study is that rare kind of program that will help one cross an elusive threshold—using the Bible effectively for prayer and spiritual enrichment. This user-friendly program will enhance any personal or group Bible study. Guaranteed to make your love of Scripture grow!"     Ronald D. Witherup, SS, biblical scholar, educator, author, and Superior General of the Sulpician Order

THRESHOLD
BIBLE STUDY

# JESUS,
# *the* MESSIANIC
# KING

PART TWO

# Matthew
# [17–28]

## STEPHEN J. BINZ

TWENTY-THIRD
PUBLICATIONS
twentythirdpublications.com

**Third printing 2018**

TWENTY-THIRD PUBLICATIONS
One Montauk Avenue, Suite 200
New London, CT 06320
(860)437-3012 or (800) 321-0411
www.twentythirdpublications.com

The Scripture passages contained herein are from the *New Revised Standard Version of the Bible*, Catholic edition. Copyright ©1989, by the Division of Christian Education of the National Council of Churches in the U.S.A. All rights reserved.

Page x (*clockwise from top*): iStockphoto/cjp; Photos.com; www.bible.ca; Photos.com; Designpics.com

The map on page x can be viewed at www.bible.ca. Copyright ©1994 by Abingdon Press. Used by permission.

ISBN 978-1-58595-816-0
Library of Congress Control Number: 2010938681
Printed in the U.S.A.

 A division of Bayard, Inc.

# Contents

# How to Use
# Threshold Bible Study

T hreshold Bible Study is a dynamic, informative, inspiring, and life-changing series that helps you learn about Scripture in a whole new way. Each
book will help you explore new dimensions of faith and discover deeper
insights for your life as a disciple of Jesus.

The threshold is a place of transition. The threshold of God's word invites you
to enter that place where God's truth, goodness, and beauty can shine into your life
and fill your mind and heart. Through the Holy Spirit, the threshold becomes holy
ground, sacred space, and graced time. God can teach you best at the threshold,
because God opens your life to his word and fills you with the Spirit of truth.

With Threshold Bible Study each topic or book of the Bible is approached in a
thematic way. You will understand and reflect on the biblical texts through over-
arching themes derived from biblical theology. Through this method, the study of
Scripture will impact your life in a unique way and transform you from within.

These books are designed for maximum flexibility. Each study is presented in
a workbook format, with sections for reading, reflecting, writing, discussing, and
praying. Each Threshold book contains thirty lessons, which you can use for your
daily study over the course of a month or which can be divided into six lessons
per week, providing a group study of six weekly sessions. These studies are ideal
for Bible study groups, small Christian communities, adult faith formation, stu-
dent groups, Sunday school, neighborhood groups, and family reading, as well as
for individual learning.

The commentary that follows each biblical passage launches your reflection on
that passage and helps you begin to see its significance within the context of your
contemporary experience. The questions following the commentary challenge
you to understand the passage more fully and apply it to your own life. Space for
writing after each question is ideal for personal study and also allows group participants to prepare for the weekly discussion. The prayer helps conclude your
study each day by integrating your learning into your relationship with God.

The method of Threshold Bible Study is rooted in the ancient tradition of *lectio
divina*, whereby studying the Bible becomes a means of deeper intimacy with

God and a transformed life. Reading and interpreting the text (*lectio*) is followed by reflective meditation on its message (*meditatio*). This reading and reflecting flows into prayer from the heart (*oratio* and *contemplatio*). In this way, one listens to God through the Scripture and then responds to God in prayer.

This ancient method assures you that Bible study is a matter of both the mind and the heart. It is not just an intellectual exercise to learn more and be able to discuss the Bible with others. It is, more importantly, a transforming experience. Reflecting on God's word, guided by the Holy Spirit, illumines the mind with wisdom and stirs the heart with zeal.

Following the personal Bible study, Threshold Bible Study offers ways to extend personal *lectio divina* into a weekly conversation with others. This communal experience will allow participants to enhance their appreciation of the message and build up a spiritual community (*collatio*). The end result will be to increase not only individual faith, but also faithful witness in the context of daily life (*operatio*).

When bringing Threshold Bible Study to a church community, try to make every effort to include as many people as possible. Many will want to study on their own; others will want to study with family, a group of friends, or a few work associates; some may want to commit themselves to share insights through a weekly conference call, daily text messaging, or an online social network; and others will want to gather weekly in established small groups.

By encouraging Threshold Bible Study and respecting the many ways people desire to make Bible study a regular part of their lives, you will widen the number of people in your church community who study the Bible regularly in whatever way they are able in their busy lives. Simply sign up people at the Sunday services and order bulk quantities for your church. Encourage people to follow the daily study as faithfully as they can through Sunday announcements, notices in parish publications, support on the church website, and other creative invitations and motivations.

Through the spiritual disciplines of Scripture reading, study, reflection, conversation, and prayer, Threshold Bible Study will help you experience God's grace more abundantly and root your life more deeply in Christ. The risen Jesus said: "Listen! I am standing at the door, knocking; if you hear my voice and open the door, I will come in to you and eat with you, and you with me" (Rev 3:20). Listen to the Word of God, open the door, and cross the threshold to an unimaginable dwelling with God!

# SUGGESTIONS FOR INDIVIDUAL STUDY

• Make your Bible reading a time of prayer. Ask for God's guidance as you read the Scriptures.

• Try to study daily, or as often as possible according to the circumstances of your life.

• Read the Bible passage carefully, trying to understand both its meaning and its personal application as you read. Some persons find it helpful to read the passage aloud.

• Read the passage in another Bible translation. Each version adds to your understanding of the original text.

• Allow the commentary to help you comprehend and apply the scriptural text. The commentary is only a beginning, not the last word on the meaning of the passage.

• After reflecting on each question, write out your responses. The very act of writing will help you clarify your thoughts, bring new insights, and amplify your understanding.

• As you reflect on your answers, think about how you can live God's word in the context of your daily life.

• Conclude each daily lesson by reading the prayer and continuing with your own prayer from the heart.

• Make sure your reflections and prayers are matters of both the mind and the heart. A true encounter with God's word is always a transforming experience.

• Choose a word or a phrase from the lesson to carry with you throughout the day as a reminder of your encounter with God's life-changing word.

• Share your learning experience with at least one other person whom you trust for additional insights and affirmation. The ideal way to share learning is in a small group that meets regularly.

# SUGGESTIONS FOR GROUP STUDY

• Meet regularly; weekly is ideal. Try to be on time and make attendance a high priority for the sake of the group. The average group meets for about an hour.

• Open each session with a prepared prayer, a song, or a reflection. Find some appropriate way to bring the group from the workaday world into a sacred time of graced sharing.

• If you have not been together before, nametags are very helpful as group members begin to become acquainted with one another.

• Spend the first session getting acquainted with one another, reading the Introduction aloud and discussing the questions that follow.

• Appoint a group facilitator to provide guidance to the discussion. The role of facilitator may rotate among members each week. The facilitator simply keeps the discussion on track; each person shares responsibility for the group. There is no need for the facilitator to be a trained teacher.

• Try to study the six lessons on your own during the week. When you have done your own reflection and written your own answers, you will be better prepared to discuss the six scriptural lessons with the group. If you have not had an opportunity to study the passages during the week, meet with the group anyway to share support and insights.

• Participate in the discussion as much as you are able, offering your thoughts, insights, feelings, and decisions. You learn by sharing with others the fruits of your study.

• Be careful not to dominate the discussion. It is important that everyone in the group be offered an equal opportunity to share the results of their work. Try to link what you say to the comments of others so that the group remains on the topic.

• When discussing your own personal thoughts or feelings, use "I" language. Be as personal and honest as appropriate and be very cautious about giving advice to others.

• Listen attentively to the other members of the group so as to learn from their insights. The words of the Bible affect each person in a different way, so a group provides a wealth of understanding for each member.

• Don't fear silence. Silence in a group is as important as silence in personal study. It allows individuals time to listen to the voice of God's Spirit and the opportunity to form their thoughts before they speak.

• Solicit several responses for each question. The thoughts of different people will build on the answers of others and will lead to deeper insights for all.

• Don't fear controversy. Differences of opinions are a sign of a healthy and honest group. If you cannot resolve an issue, continue on, agreeing to disagree. There is probably some truth in each viewpoint.

• Discuss the questions that seem most important for the group. There is no need to cover all the questions in the group session.

• Realize that some questions about the Bible cannot be resolved, even by experts. Don't get stuck on some issue for which there are no clear answers.

• Whatever is said in the group is said in confidence and should be regarded as such.

• Pray as a group in whatever way feels comfortable. Pray for the members of your group throughout the week.


## Schedule for Group Study

Session 1: Introduction                 Date: _____

Session 2: Lessons 1–6                  Date: _____

Session 3: Lessons 7–12                 Date: _____

Session 4: Lessons 13–18                Date: _____

Session 5: Lessons 19–24                Date: _____

Session 6: Lessons 25–30                Date: _____

The Gospel According to
# MATTHEW

...count of the genealogy of Jesus
...essiah, the son of David, the
...am.
...m was the father of I...
...er of J...

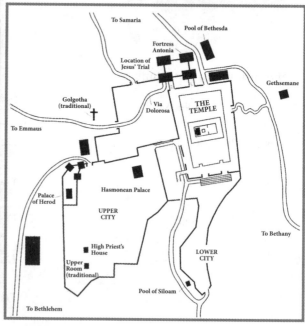

"Look, your king is coming to you, humble,
and mounted on a donkey." Matt 21:5

# Jesus, the Messianic King (Part 2)

In the second half of the gospel, Matthew continues to portray Jesus as the promised king who will bring salvation to his people. Yet, as Jesus continues to move in the direction of Jerusalem and toward his passion and death, his role as Israel's royal Messiah is linked more and more to his humble service and self-sacrificing love. The gospel increasingly demonstrates that the inaugurator of God's kingdom is the suffering Messiah who will give his life to bring salvation to the world.

In the final scene of chapter 16, Peter had proclaimed Jesus as "the Messiah, the Son of the living God." While Jesus praised Peter's response and designated Peter as the foundation of his church, Jesus also indicated that Peter had much to learn about what it means to call Jesus the messianic Son and to follow in his way. At this turning point of the gospel, Jesus began to tell his disciples that he must suffer greatly, be killed, and then be raised to life. He also taught his followers that they must take up their cross in imitation of him, and that they must lose their own lives in order to find true life.

The presentation of Jesus as the messianic King, which Matthew has developed throughout the gospel, moves toward its climax as Jesus approaches the royal city of Jerusalem and moves toward the cross. Jesus' triumphal entry into Jerusalem near the end of his life is the act of a king. In describing the final judgment, Jesus portrays himself as a king who sits on a glorious throne, separating those on his right hand from those on his left. When put on trial as "King of the Jews," Jesus is mocked with a scarlet robe and a crown of thorns. Then, as he is publicly ridiculed with a signboard over the cross proclaiming him king, the religious leaders challenge him to prove his royal power as "the King of Israel" by coming down from the cross. Of course the irony of these scenes of Christ's passion is the fact that Jesus truly is their messianic king, though he does not manifest his royal power with spectacular acts. All of his words and deeds are oriented toward making known God's kingdom and submitting to his will.

As the gospel proceeds toward its pinnacle, Matthew continues to express his central theme: The saving history of Israel has reached its purpose and goal in Jesus the Messiah. As the fulfillment of the Torah and the prophets of Israel, Jesus brings all the images and institutions of the Hebrew Scriptures to their climactic expression in himself and the kingdom he has inaugurated. As Israel's Messiah, he is the full embodiment of the ancient kings, prophets, and priests. He is Israel's greatest king, the Son of David as well as the Lord of David, and the king wiser than Solomon. He is the anticipated prophet like Moses, greater than Elijah, more obedient than Jonah, the one for whom John the Baptist prepared the way. As the bearer of God's kingdom, he is Lord of the Sabbath and the final temple of God's presence.

Matthew's gospel shows the age of promise giving way to the age of fulfillment. As Jesus fulfills the covenants made with Abraham, Moses, and David, he inaugurates the long-awaited new covenant. This new and everlasting relationship with God is accomplished in the passion and death of Jesus and ratified in his blood (26:28). It is the climax of God's eternal plan to bring salvation to the house of Israel and all the Gentile nations.

## Reflection and Discussion

• What can I anticipate as characteristics of the second half of Matthew's gospel?

• What irony is expressed in Matthew's passion narrative when Jesus is mocked as Israel's king?

## Conflicts over the True Inheritance of Ancient Israel

Though Matthew was a Jew and his gospel was written to a community of mostly Jewish followers of Jesus, there are signs throughout the gospel of tensions with other Jewish groups. On the one hand, the gospel emphasizes the Jewish tradition of Jesus and his disciples, insisting on the continuity of Jesus with the Old Testament and demonstrating that Jesus and his disciples followed the teachings given through Moses. On the other hand, the gospel is marked with debates and conflicts between Jesus and many of the Jewish leaders of his day, the Pharisees and Sadducees, the chief priests, scribes, and elders. As the action of the gospel moves toward Jerusalem and enters the confines of the temple, the confrontation becomes increasingly intense.

Matthew's gospel demonstrates that Jesus and his divine mission are the culmination of the history of salvation manifested through ancient Israel. Jesus has completed the law and the prophets, inaugurated the long-awaited kingdom, and will lead the community of faith to the end of the age. Because of the treacherous mismanagement of God's people by their leaders and the attempts of these leaders to turn the people against Jesus, Matthew's gospel portrays Jesus as relentless in his criticism of them. In fact, the gospel suggests that the terrors of the Jewish war with Rome in AD 66-70, resulting in the destruction of Jerusalem and its temple, are divine judgment upon the city's unfaithful leaders and the generation that fell under their sway.

This intense verbal conflict in the gospel's second half reflects the wrenching separation between Matthew's Jewish-Christian community and the form of rabbinical Judaism being developed after the destruction of Jerusalem and its temple. Both forms of Judaism claimed to be the legitimate heir of the tradition of ancient Israel. As we read the gospel today, this intense conflict between Jesus and his religious opponents must be read within its historical context. This was a debate between two groups of Jews, not a conflict between Jesus and Jews, or between the Christian church and Judaism. Jesus and his disciples, as well as Matthew and the community in which he wrote the gospel, were all Jews, seeking to be faithful to the tradition in which God had led them. When the Gospel of Matthew is read in later non-Jewish cultures, it can easily be misinterpreted as a Christian polemic against Jews, as history has sadly demonstrated. The modern reader of the gospel, then, has the responsibility to consider the original context of the gospel, lest it fuel the kind of anti-Judaism that has so dreadfully distorted Christian history.

## Reflection and Discussion

• Why is Matthew's gospel often described as the most Jewish of the four gospels?

• Why is it so critically important today that readers interpret this gospel while taking into account its original Jewish context?

## The Presence of Jesus with his Church until the End

Matthew's gospel shows great interest in the church, the organized community of disciples continuing the mission of Jesus in the world. His is the only gospel to use the word "church" (*ekklesia* in Greek) and much of the gospel is concerned with teaching members of the church how life should be lived within the community. The announcement of God's kingdom summons disciples in surprising ways from unlikely sources, so that this network of lives joined together in Christ consists of tax collectors and sinners, women and men, Jews and Gentiles.

The whole gospel, highlighted by the five prominent sermons of Jesus, seems to be written to meet the catechetical needs of the growing community. The sermon on the mount (Mt 5–7), the sermon to the apostles (Mt 10), the sermon on the kingdom (Mt 13), the sermon on leadership (Mt 18), and the sermon on the last things (Mt 24–25) instruct the church on how to live within the new covenant until the end of the age. Jesus educates his present and future disciples on how to be humble, to seek out those who stray, to settle disputes, and offer forgiveness. In this context, Jesus' fierce criticism of the religious leaders is not so much an attack on Jewish opponents as a warning to the leaders of the church. The hypocrites and blind guides, who do not practice what they preach, who fail to offer mercy and refuse to listen to the prophets of their day, are not worthy to lead God's people. Unworthy leaders will leave the church as desolate as Jerusalem and its temple.

The church is not the kingdom of God, but the kingdom is present in the church because of the abiding presence of the church's Lord. Jesus is with his church when the storm strikes on the waters, when his disciples are welcomed or rejected when preaching his kingdom, and wherever two or three are gathered in his name. To emphasize the divine presence of Jesus with his church, Matthew frames his entire gospel with this theme. In the first chapter, Jesus is named Emmanuel, which means "God is with us" (1:23). In the last verse of the gospel, the risen Jesus assures his community with the pledge, "I am with you always, to the end of the age" (28:20). As a people of the kingdom living in the new age of salvation, the church is able to live in the world with confident trust as it embodies the living presence of its risen Lord.

## Reflection and Discussion

• In what way is the Gospel of Matthew intended to be a pastoral tool for the church's preaching and teaching?

• What seems to be the relationship between the church and the kingdom of God according to Matthew's gospel?

## The Concluding Chapters of Matthew's Gospel

This second half of Matthew's gospel begins with the vision of Jesus' glorious transfiguration and ends with his wondrous resurrection appearance to the disciples. In the scene of the transfiguration, the disciples fall to the ground and are overcome with fear. Jesus then commands them to "get up and do not be afraid," and they follow him down the mountain to his destiny in Jerusalem. In the final scene of the gospel, Jesus appears to his disciples on another mountain as they bow down to worship him. Jesus then commands them to go forth and evangelize all the nations, assuring them that he is with them always.

Sandwiched between these glorious scenes of transfiguration and resurrection, Jesus teaches his disciples how to live as his church. The journey to Jerusalem and the passion and death of Jesus are narrated in the light of the glorified messianic king. The cross on which he died, the cross that his disciples must carry in his footsteps, is illumined with glory. It is in the light of this cross, with all its pain and all its hope, that the church is called to live in faithful service and watchful expectation. As the historical Jesus formed his disciples to be his church, the Jesus of Matthew's gospel forms the church throughout time to live in the time between his resurrection and his return at the end of the age.

In every period of Christian history, the Gospel of Matthew has brought direction and hope for Christ's disciples, inviting them into an ever deeper relationship with Jesus, who promises to remain always with his church. As we continue our study of this gospel, we will experience the saving news of Jesus as it was experienced by that early community of Jews and Gentiles to which Matthew addressed his gospel. As the gospel equipped those ancient

Christians with the teaching of Jesus the Messiah so they could spread the message of the kingdom to all the nations, the gospel will prepare us through the transforming experience of Jesus Christ to be bearers of the good news in the world today.

## Reflection and Discussion

• In what way do I want to be formed as a disciple of Jesus as I study the Gospel of Matthew?

• How does the promise of Jesus to remain always with his church affect the way that I study this gospel?

## Prayer

*Father of our Lord Jesus, you glorified your Son in his transfiguration and resurrection. May the light of his glory brighten my path as I seek to follow in the way of discipleship. As I travel with Jesus to Jerusalem through the path of this gospel, stir up within me a deep desire to know him more fully and to listen carefully to his teachings. Help me to understand how you have brought your ancient promises to fulfillment and opened salvation to all the nations of the world. Form me as a vital member of Christ's church and show me how to make my life a testimony to the presence of your kingdom.*

# SUGGESTIONS FOR FACILITATORS, GROUP SESSION 1

1. If the group is meeting for the first time, or if there are newcomers joining the group, it is helpful to provide name tags.

2. Distribute the books to the members of the group.

3. You may want to ask the participants to introduce themselves and tell the group a bit about themselves.

4. Ask one or more of these introductory questions:
   • What drew you to join this group?
   • What is your biggest fear in beginning this Bible study?
   • How is beginning this study like a "threshold" for you?

5. You may want to pray this prayer as a group:

*Come upon us, Holy Spirit, to enlighten and guide us as we continue this study of Matthew's gospel. You inspired the writers of the Scriptures to reveal your presence throughout the history of salvation. This inspired word has the power to convert our hearts and change our lives. Fill our hearts with desire, trust, and confidence as you shine the light of your truth within us. Motivate us to read the Scriptures and give us a deeper love for God's word each day. Bless us during this session and throughout the coming week with the fire of your love.*

6. Read the Introduction aloud, pausing at each question for discussion. Group members may wish to write the insights of the group as each question is discussed. Encourage several members of the group to respond to each question.

7. Don't feel compelled to finish the complete Introduction during the session. It is better to allow sufficient time to talk about the questions raised than to rush to the end. Group members may read any remaining sections on their own after the group meeting.

8. Instruct group members to read the first six lessons on their own during the six days before the next group meeting. They should write out their own answers to the questions as preparation for next week's group discussion.

9. Fill in the date for each group meeting under "Schedule for Group Study."

10. Conclude by praying aloud together the prayer at the end of the Introduction.

He was transfigured before them, and his face shone like the sun, and his clothes became dazzling white. Suddenly there appeared to them Moses and Elijah, talking with him. Matt 17:2–3

# The Transfiguration of Jesus

**MATTHEW 17:1–13** ¹*Six days later, Jesus took with him Peter and James and his brother John and led them up a high mountain, by themselves. ²And he was transfigured before them, and his face shone like the sun, and his clothes became dazzling white. ³Suddenly there appeared to them Moses and Elijah, talking with him. ⁴Then Peter said to Jesus, "Lord, it is good for us to be here; if you wish, I will make three dwellings here, one for you, one for Moses, and one for Elijah." ⁵While he was still speaking, suddenly a bright cloud overshadowed them, and from the cloud a voice said, "This is my Son, the Beloved; with him I am well pleased; listen to him!" ⁶When the disciples heard this, they fell to the ground and were overcome by fear. ⁷But Jesus came and touched them, saying, "Get up and do not be afraid." ⁸And when they looked up, they saw no one except Jesus himself alone.*

*⁹As they were coming down the mountain, Jesus ordered them, "Tell no one about the vision until after the Son of Man has been raised from the dead." ¹⁰And the disciples asked him, "Why, then, do the scribes say that Elijah must come first?" ¹¹He replied, "Elijah is indeed coming and will restore all things; ¹²but I tell you that Elijah has already come, and they did not recognize him, but they did to him whatever they pleased. So also the Son of Man is about to suffer at their hands."* [13]*Then the disciples understood that he was speaking to them about John the Baptist.*

T hough the glorious transfiguration of Jesus comes midway through the gospel, its wondrous nature is not completely unanticipated. Jesus came into the world in a marvelous way, and his ministry began when his Father acknowledged him at his baptism, "This is my Son, the Beloved." Jesus has performed great deeds of compassion marking the closeness of God's kingdom and has demonstrated in his teaching that he is the definitive interpreter of Israel's Torah. He has demonstrated his authority over the sea and provided food for thousands. The transfiguration of Jesus offers the disciples an even fuller glimpse of who Jesus is and what he will do.

The transfiguration event recalls God's presentation of the Torah to Moses in Exodus 24 and 34. The high mountain recalls the heights of Mount Sinai, where God was manifested to Moses. The description of the countenance of Jesus, "his face shone like the sun," evokes the report of the face of Moses, which "shone because he had been talking with God" (Exod 34:29). The mention of Peter, James, and John accompanying Jesus reminds the reader of the companions of Moses on the mountain, Aaron, Nadab, and Abihu (Exod 25:1). The interval of six days and the Father's voice from the cloud recall the cloud that covered Mount Sinai for six days and the voice of God that called to Moses on the seventh day (Exod 24:16). As Moses and Elijah become part of the vision of the transfigured Jesus, the scene incorporates the full sweep of Israel's saving history. Moses and Elijah represent "the law and the prophets" and Jesus is the final fulfillment of Israel's messianic hopes.

Peter's instincts are correct when he offers to erect three "dwellings" on the spot (verse 4). The word indicates the temporary, makeshift shelters erected during the Jewish Feast of Sukkoth to remember Israel's forty-year journey through the desert. Peter's remembrance of the saving path of Exodus is a reminder that the disciples are still on the way with Jesus. As Moses and Elijah prepared his way, Jesus is preparing Peter, James, and John to travel with him to Jerusalem and to continue his way, the journey that leads to the cross. Along that way, Jesus will have much to teach his disciples about what it means to call Jesus the Messiah and Son of God.

After confirming that Jesus is indeed his beloved Son, God's voice from the cloud says, "Listen to him" (verse 5). As Peter, James, and John continue the journey with Jesus to Jerusalem, they must keep listening to what Jesus teaches them and live by those teachings. Listening to Jesus is the way to follow in his footsteps: listening to the word of God that transfigures sinners into forgiven and redeemed people, that transfigures sick and disabled bodies into healed and whole beings, that transfigures bread and wine into his body and blood, that transfigures suffering and death into resurrected life.

## Reflection and Discussion

• Jesus describes this encounter as a "vision," a God-given ability to visualize what is ordinarily imperceptible to mortal beings. Why is this holy and fascinating vision so difficult to describe? What aspects strike me the most?

• Why did Jesus show his transfigured glory to his disciples at the beginning of their journey to Jerusalem? What keeps me engaged and motivated along the path of discipleship?

## Prayer

*Transfigured Lord, I want to stay with you on the mountain, but you call me to descend with you to life's valleys. Help me to see your glory shining through life's difficult moments. Teach me to listen to you so that I may obey and follow in the way you desire for my life.*

"Truly I tell you, if you have faith the size of a mustard seed,
you will say to this mountain, 'Move from here to there,' and it will move;
and nothing will be impossible for you." Matt 17:20

# Valuable Lessons for the Disciples

**MATTHEW 17:14–27** [14]*When they came to the crowd, a man came to him, knelt before him,* [15]*and said, "Lord, have mercy on my son, for he is an epileptic and he suffers terribly; he often falls into the fire and often into the water.* [16]*And I brought him to your disciples, but they could not cure him."* [17]*Jesus answered, "You faithless and perverse generation, how much longer must I be with you? How much longer must I put up with you? Bring him here to me."* [18]*And Jesus rebuked the demon, and it came out of him, and the boy was cured instantly.* [19]*Then the disciples came to Jesus privately and said, "Why could we not cast it out?"* [20]*He said to them, "Because of your little faith. For truly I tell you, if you have faith the size of a mustard seed, you will say to this mountain, 'Move from here to there,' and it will move; and nothing will be impossible for you."*

[22]*As they were gathering in Galilee, Jesus said to them, "The Son of Man is going to be betrayed into human hands,* [23]*and they will kill him, and on the third day he will be raised." And they were greatly distressed.*

[24]*When they reached Capernaum, the collectors of the temple tax came to Peter and said, "Does your teacher not pay the temple tax?"* [25]*He said, "Yes, he does." And when he came home, Jesus spoke of it first, asking, "What do you*

*think, Simon? From whom do kings of the earth take toll or tribute? From their children or from others?"* ²⁶*When Peter said, "From others," Jesus said to him, "Then the children are free.* ²⁷*However, so that we do not give offense to them, go to the sea and cast a hook; take the first fish that comes up; and when you open its mouth, you will find a coin; take that and give it to them for you and me."*

While Jesus was on the mountain with Peter, James, and John, a man had brought his son to the remaining disciples and asked them to cure the boy (verse 16). His son suffered severely from seizures that would often occur near cooking fires or bodies of water, a form of what would be diagnosed today as epilepsy. Though Jesus had given his twelve disciples the authority to drive out unclean spirits and to cure disease and illnesses, they were not able to heal the boy. In this first instance in the gospel describing an opportunity for the disciples to exercise their healing power, they fail.

Jesus is exasperated with both the crowd and his disciples, and he chastises them in language that echoes the judgment of Moses on the people of Israel: "a perverse and crooked generation" (Deut 32:5). The crowd expects miracles from Jesus but does not grasp his identity and his mission. The disciples are unable to do what Jesus had empowered them to do. Jesus' questions, "how much longer?" (verse 17) have a particular urgency because Jesus is about to begin his journey to Jerusalem where he will suffer and die (verses 22–23). There is not much time left for his disciples to start acting like true and faithful disciples.

Jesus' cure of the boy is recounted in a few words, but the purpose of the narrative is highlighted in what happens next. When the disciples were in private with Jesus, they asked him why they were unable to drive out the demon that afflicted the boy. Jesus answered, "Because of your little faith" (verse 20). Jesus had previously described his disciples as having little faith when they became terrified at the storm on the sea (8:26), when Peter began to sink while walking on the water (14:31), and when they worried about whether they would receive their daily provisions (6:30; 16:8). They were not completely without faith, but their faith faltered when put to the test.

Jesus challenges his disciples with two hyperboles: the minuscule size of their faith, "a mustard seed," and the huge potential of their faith, moving a mountain (verse 20). When Jesus says, "Nothing will be impossible for you," he is referring to the mission he has given his disciples. There is no limit to what can be accomplished through faith. With God all things are possible. Faith leads disciples into the realm of the impossible, just as faith led Peter out of the boat to walk on the water.

The next lesson for the disciples concerns the annual temple tax that was assessed on every adult Jewish man for the support of the temple (verse 24). Jesus' brief parable states that kings do not levy taxes on their children, but on others. Likewise, Jesus and his disciples, who are God's children, are not required to pay for the upkeep of their Father's house. Jesus agrees that he and Peter should pay the tax, but not out of obligation. Jesus' teaching that "the children are free" means that the actions of Jesus disciples should be motivated out of internal desire and free choice rather than the burden of obligation. Jesus' instructions about how Peter would find the coin to pay the tax is a colorful way of illustrating the fact that God provides for the needs of his children when they trust in him.

## Reflection and Discussion

• How do I understand the promise of Jesus that a mustard seed of faith can move a mountain?

• When do I find myself with "little faith"? When has Jesus guided me into the realm of the impossible?

## Prayer

*Son of God, you have invited me to share in your mission and you guide me into the realm of the impossible. Give me the seed of genuine faith so that I will trust in you and not fail in times of testing.*

> If a shepherd has a hundred sheep, and one of them has gone astray,
> does he not leave the ninety-nine on the mountains
> and go in search of the one that went astray?
>
> Matt 18:12

# Pastoral Leadership within Community

**MATTHEW 18:1–20** ¹*At that time the disciples came to Jesus and asked, "Who is the greatest in the kingdom of heaven?" ²He called a child, whom he put among them, ³and said, "Truly I tell you, unless you change and become like children, you will never enter the kingdom of heaven. ⁴Whoever becomes humble like this child is the greatest in the kingdom of heaven. ⁵Whoever welcomes one such child in my name welcomes me.*

⁶*"If any of you put a stumbling block before one of these little ones who believe in me, it would be better for you if a great millstone were fastened around your neck and you were drowned in the depth of the sea. ⁷Woe to the world because of stumbling blocks! Occasions for stumbling are bound to come, but woe to the one by whom the stumbling block comes!*

⁸*"If your hand or your foot causes you to stumble, cut it off and throw it away; it is better for you to enter life maimed or lame than to have two hands or two feet and to be thrown into the eternal fire. ⁹And if your eye causes you to stumble, tear it out and throw it away; it is better for you to enter life with one eye than to have two eyes and to be thrown into the hell of fire.*

$^{10}$"Take care that you do not despise one of these little ones; for, I tell you, in heaven their angels continually see the face of my Father in heaven. $^{12}$What do you think? If a shepherd has a hundred sheep, and one of them has gone astray, does he not leave the ninety-nine on the mountains and go in search of the one that went astray? $^{13}$And if he finds it, truly I tell you, he rejoices over it more than over the ninety-nine that never went astray. $^{14}$So it is not the will of your Father in heaven that one of these little ones should be lost.

$^{15}$"If another member of the church sins against you, go and point out the fault when the two of you are alone. If the member listens to you, you have regained that one. $^{16}$But if you are not listened to, take one or two others along with you, so that every word may be confirmed by the evidence of two or three witnesses. $^{17}$If the member refuses to listen to them, tell it to the church; and if the offender refuses to listen even to the church, let such a one be to you as a Gentile and a tax collector. $^{18}$Truly I tell you, whatever you bind on earth will be bound in heaven, and whatever you loose on earth will be loosed in heaven. $^{19}$Again, truly I tell you, if two of you agree on earth about anything you ask, it will be done for you by my Father in heaven. $^{20}$For where two or three are gathered in my name, I am there among them."

The fourth of Jesus' five major sermons in the gospel is prompted by a question from his disciples: "Who is the greatest in the kingdom of heaven?" People have a natural desire to be prominent and seen as important; however, Jesus demonstrates that greatness in God's kingdom undercuts what might be expected in a worldly realm. As Jesus addresses his sermon to those who will have leadership responsibility within the church, he dramatically illustrates his response by placing a child in the midst of his listeners. A child in the culture of the time was one without status or power. Greatness, then, in God's kingdom means becoming like children, shedding pretensions, and living in a spirit of humility (verse 4). Jesus then adds that disciples must not only become like children, but they must also welcome and serve those who are powerless like children (verse 5). Lavishing care on these little ones is the way to true leadership within the church.

As Jesus continues his discourse, he instructs his disciples about life within his church. Leaders must take great care not to place obstacles in the way of the "little ones," those who are the most weak and vulnerable members of the community (verse 6). The "stumbling block" represents some sinful or scandalous attitude or behavior that harms the faith of these little ones. Jesus uses a strong metaphor to convey the serious consequences of causing those who are weak in faith to sin or lose hope. A millstone is a large grinding stone turned by a donkey. A millstone around one's neck would ensure a rapid descent to the bottom of the sea. Though scandals are bound to occur in our sin-marred world, those who cause them are on a path to destruction (verse 7). Continuing with bold language, Jesus urges disciples to deal radically with sinful tendencies that could cause harm to others (verses 8–9). Though these images of amputation and gouging are grotesque, the pain of eternal loss of God's kingdom is far worse.

The pastors of the church must always seek out the weak and errant members. Through the parable of the lost sheep, Jesus emphasizes the extraordinary lengths a pastor should go to in recovering one who goes astray (verse 12). Those who shepherd the church should rejoice greatly over the recovery of one missing member because the Father in heaven does not wish any of the little ones to be lost.

Finally, Jesus offers a three-step process for confronting a fellow disciple who sins within the community (verses 15–17). The first step is a private conversation directly with the offender. This attempt to persuade the wrongdoer averts bitter gossip and seeks reconciliation. If no progress is made, then two or three witnesses should be introduced into the process. If this small group of peers fails to produce reconciliation, then the case should be brought before the whole community of the church. The purpose of the process is always to restore the offender to the community. If all these attempts fail, then the wrongdoer must be treated like "a Gentile and a tax-collector." In the Jewish arena, these represent an outsider and a sinner. However, considering Jesus' unrelenting compassion for Gentiles and tax collectors, perhaps he is saying that his church should never give up on anyone. Even if the church must exclude a wayward member, it must always be the goal to seek repentance from the wrongdoer. The pastoral concern of the community for an errant member never completely ends.

Jesus teaches that the church, the community gathered in his name, is invested with his saving presence and power. It has the authority to "bind" and "loose," to declare what is permitted and not permitted, to exclude one from the community or to reconcile one with the community. Most importantly,

Jesus assures the leaders that wherever the church is gathered, even when only two or three of its members are present, "I am there among them."

## Reflection and Discussion

• Why does Jesus begin his sermon on leadership by placing a child in the midst of his disciples? Why would a child be such a powerful demonstration of the attitude and behavior required of church leaders?

• Why does Jesus use such harsh language to describe the consequences of causing a weak member of the church to trip and fall? What should I get rid of to prevent the scandal of one of God's little ones?

• What is the purpose of enlisting two or three others to help work out a difficulty with another person? How have I experienced the presence of Jesus where two or three are gathered in his name?

## Prayer

*Lord Jesus, I know that you are with your church whenever we gather in your name. Help me to realize that I am invoking your saving presence whenever I seek to reconcile with another member of your church. Give me your compassion and mercy toward others.*

**"I forgave you all that debt because you pleaded with me. Should you not have had mercy on your fellow slave, as I had mercy on you?"** Matt 18:32–33

# The Necessity of Forgiveness

**MATTHEW 18:21–35** ²¹*Then Peter came and said to him, "Lord, if another member of the church sins against me, how often should I forgive? As many as seven times?" ²²Jesus said to him, "Not seven times, but, I tell you, seventy-seven times.*

²³*"For this reason the kingdom of heaven may be compared to a king who wished to settle accounts with his slaves. ²⁴When he began the reckoning, one who owed him ten thousand talents was brought to him; ²⁵and, as he could not pay, his lord ordered him to be sold, together with his wife and children and all his possessions, and payment to be made. ²⁶So the slave fell on his knees before him, saying, 'Have patience with me, and I will pay you everything.' ²⁷And out of pity for him, the lord of that slave released him and forgave him the debt. ²⁸But that same slave, as he went out, came upon one of his fellow slaves who owed him a hundred denarii; and seizing him by the throat, he said, 'Pay what you owe.' ²⁹Then his fellow slave fell down and pleaded with him, 'Have patience with me, and I will pay you.' ³⁰But he refused; then he went and threw him into prison until he would pay the debt. ³¹When his fellow slaves saw what had happened, they were greatly distressed, and they went*

*and reported to their lord all that had taken place.* [32]*Then his lord summoned him and said to him, 'You wicked slave! I forgave you all that debt because you pleaded with me.* [33]*Should you not have had mercy on your fellow slave, as I had mercy on you?'* [34]*And in anger his lord handed him over to be tortured until he would pay his entire debt.* [35]*So my heavenly Father will also do to every one of you, if you do not forgive your brother or sister from your heart."*

Throughout his sermon on church leadership, Jesus has spoken about the community of his disciples with utmost mercy and tenderness. He has compared them to humble children, little ones, lost sheep, and brothers and sisters. Though confrontation and discipline are often necessary, the goal is always reconciliation and returning the strays to the fold. Assuring the church of his ongoing presence, Jesus demonstrates that its sacred work must always be permeated with humility, familial love, and a passion for forgiveness and reconciliation.

In this familial context, Peter asks Jesus about the extent of forgiveness. Perhaps he is concerned to clarify the three-step process Jesus has just described for reconciling errant members of the church. Peter thinks that surely seven times is adequate to forgive. Jesus' answer, however, indicates that forgiveness must be unending. His response, "seventy-seven times," alludes to the response of Lamech, a descendant of Cain, who boasts that he will exact overwhelming vengeance on anyone who dares to attack him: "If Cain is avenged sevenfold, truly Lamech seventy-sevenfold" (Gen 4:24). Jesus presents forgiveness as the polar opposite of revenge. Disciples must renounce the instinct to retaliate against someone who repeatedly wrongs them and offer unlimited forgiveness.

The impact of this parable of Jesus is found first in the contrast between the huge debt owed by the slave, a massive amount that could never possibly be repaid, and the rather small debt owed to the slave. The parable's effect is found next in the contrast between the king's deeply emotional and big-hearted decision to forgive the slave's debt completely and that same slave's brutal and merciless response to his fellow slave. Because the slave had already been forgiven an astounding and unpayable obligation by his king, he should have lived his life in memory of that amazing grace.

This illustration of Jesus' teaching shows us that we must be constant in our forgiving because God's forgiving mercy toward us knows no bounds. Each of us is that slave who owed a staggering amount, but whose debt was pardoned by the merciful king. If such a debt has been forgiven for us by God, how generous should we be in forgiving others? Peter's question addressed a human problem from a human perspective. This parable of the kingdom grounds forgiveness in the very nature of God.

Jesus urges disciples to "forgive your brother or sister from your heart." Although we have been lovingly forgiven by our God, we can only open our lives to receive that forgiveness when we forgive others from our hearts. As we forgive one another, we allow that tremendous forgiveness of God to take hold of our lives and renew us from within. God's forgiveness then overflows from our lives into Christ's church.

## Reflection and Discussion

• Why is forgiveness important both for the psychological health of individuals and for the health of communities?

• In what way does Jesus desire his church to be an instrument of forgiveness? How could I be a better channel of God's forgiveness?

## Prayer

*Lord Jesus, you call me to forgive my brothers and sisters from the heart. Make me a channel of your healing mercy and lead your church to be an instrument of your forgiveness in the world today.*

"Let the little children come to me, and do not stop them;
for it is to such as these that the kingdom of heaven belongs."

Matt 19:14

# Teachings on Marriage, Celibacy, and Children

MATTHEW 19:1–15 *¹When Jesus had finished saying these things, he left Galilee and went to the region of Judea beyond the Jordan. ²Large crowds followed him, and he cured them there.*

*³Some Pharisees came to him, and to test him they asked, "Is it lawful for a man to divorce his wife for any cause?" ⁴He answered, "Have you not read that the one who made them at the beginning 'made them male and female,' ⁵and said, 'For this reason a man shall leave his father and mother and be joined to his wife, and the two shall become one flesh'? ⁶So they are no longer two, but one flesh. Therefore what God has joined together, let no one separate." ⁷They said to him, "Why then did Moses command us to give a certificate of dismissal and to divorce her?" ⁸He said to them, "It was because you were so hard-hearted that Moses allowed you to divorce your wives, but from the beginning it was not so. ⁹And I say to you, whoever divorces his wife, except for unchastity, and marries another commits adultery."*

*¹⁰His disciples said to him, "If such is the case of a man with his wife, it is better not to marry." ¹¹But he said to them, "Not everyone can accept this teaching, but only those to whom it is given. ¹²For there are eunuchs who have been so from birth, and there are eunuchs who have been made eunuchs by others, and there are eunuchs who have made themselves eunuchs for the sake of the kingdom of heaven. Let anyone accept this who can."*

¹³*Then little children were being brought to him in order that he might lay his hands on them and pray. The disciples spoke sternly to those who brought them;* ¹⁴*but Jesus said, "Let the little children come to me, and do not stop them; for it is to such as these that the kingdom of heaven belongs."* ¹⁵*And he laid his hands on them and went on his way.*

A s Jesus moves southward, from Galilee into Judea, his confrontation with the religious leaders intensifies. His debate with the Pharisees on marriage and divorce leads to Jesus correcting the disciples on their views of marriage and children. In this focus on the family, Jesus teaches about life choices and domestic issues in relationship to God's kingdom.

Though the gospel has already included Jesus' teaching on the permanency of marriage in the sermon on the mount (5:31–32), this discussion centers on the appropriate grounds for divorce. Since the law of Moses permitted divorce in Deuteronomy 24:1, the rabbis had debated whether it is "lawful for a man to divorce his wife for any cause," or whether only certain circumstances justified divorce (verse 3). The Pharisees decide to "test" Jesus, trying to demonstrate that he contradicts Moses.

Jesus responds to the test question not by referring to the permission for divorce given by Moses in Deuteronomy, but by reaching back to the creation of man and woman in the opening pages of Genesis. God's creation of male and female, and God's joining of husband and wife as "one flesh," express God's original intent for marriage (Gen 1:27; 2:24). The identity of the couple as children of their parents is altered, and their primary identity as husband and wife becomes permanent. The teaching of Moses that allowed a man to divorce his wife is a concession to human sinfulness, not God's plan and desire for marriage. Jesus exhorts his listeners, "Therefore what God has joined together, let no one separate" (verse 6).

The exception clause in Jesus' prohibition of divorce, translated here as "except for unchastity" (verse 9) has long been debated. The clause could refer to sexual infidelity, breaking the "one flesh" description of marriage. However, Jesus' teachings on forgiveness indicate that the deep wounds of infidelity can be healed by God's reconciling love in Christ. The exception clause probably refers to an unlawful marriage to a close relative, a practice tolerated by Gentile culture but not by Judaism or the church. In any case, since the clause is found only in Matthew's gospel, it seems that Matthew inserted the exception in order to apply Jesus' teaching to the situation of the church he addressed. He indicates that dissolving such an unlawful marriage is not a violation of Jesus' prohibition of divorce.

Though the law of Moses only allows the husband to initiate divorce, Jesus' teaching implies a basic equality between men and women in marriage. A husband who divorces his wife commits adultery against her. For women in the time of Jesus, his stricter teaching on divorce safeguarded women from being cast aside and placed in a vulnerable social and economic situation. In the same way, applying Jesus' teaching to our contemporary situation must take into account Jesus' primary concern for the well-being of both partners within the community.

Thinking that Jesus' teachings on marriage are overly restrictive, the disciples suggest that perhaps "it is better not to marry" (verse 10). Jesus takes their conclusion as the occasion to complement his teaching on marriage with a teaching on remaining single. While maintaining marriage as God's usual intention for men and women, Jesus suggests that God gives to some the grace to remain unmarried (verse 11). Jesus uses the image of the eunuch as a graphic comparison to explain why some do not marry: some are born eunuchs, some are made eunuchs, and some choose to figuratively become eunuchs by forsaking marriage and living celibately. Such a choice seems to have been made by Jeremiah, John the Baptist, and Jesus for the sake of the mission they had been given by God. Both marriage and celibacy are equally demanding, and neither of these lifestyles can be lived well without God's calling and grace.

The disciples' dismissive view of Jesus' teachings on marriage and their desire to dismiss the children from the scope of Jesus' concerns indicate their commonplace view of family life (verse 13). Jesus tells his disciples never to keep children from coming to him, because they exemplify the central value of the kingdom. Jesus elevates marriage and children by showing how they are centrally important in God's reign. The kingdom of heaven extends to our most intimate relationships and commitments: the single life, celibacy, marriage, parenthood, and childhood.

## Reflection and Discussion

• In what way do these teachings of Jesus elevate the importance of the life-style choices I have made?

• While the principles of gospel teachings may be clear in the abstract, they are often confusing in specific situations. Why do we need a church to help us discern God's will and understand how to live the teachings of Jesus?

• Who are the best witnesses for me of living marriage, celibacy, or parenthood "for the sake of the kingdom of heaven"?

## Prayer

*Lord Jesus, I know that it is easier to profess your teachings than to live them. Give me the wisdom to discern my vocational choices, confidence in your grace to follow, and generosity to live out my choices for the sake of the kingdom.*

"Everyone who has left houses or brothers or sisters
or father or mother or children or fields, for my name's sake,
will receive a hundredfold, and will inherit eternal life." Matt 19:29

# Discipleship, Possessions, and True Rewards

**MATTHEW 19:16–30** ¹⁶*Then someone came to him and said, "Teacher, what good deed must I do to have eternal life?" ¹⁷And he said to him, "Why do you ask me about what is good? There is only one who is good. If you wish to enter into life, keep the commandments." ¹⁸He said to him, "Which ones?" And Jesus said, "You shall not murder; You shall not commit adultery; You shall not steal; You shall not bear false witness; ¹⁹Honor your father and mother; also, You shall love your neighbor as yourself." ²⁰The young man said to him, "I have kept all these; what do I still lack?" ²¹Jesus said to him, "If you wish to be perfect, go, sell your possessions, and give the money to the poor, and you will have treasure in heaven; then come, follow me." ²²When the young man heard this word, he went away grieving, for he had many possessions.*

*²³Then Jesus said to his disciples, "Truly I tell you, it will be hard for a rich person to enter the kingdom of heaven. ²⁴Again I tell you, it is easier for a camel to go through the eye of a needle than for someone who is rich to enter the kingdom of God." ²⁵When the disciples heard this, they were greatly astounded and said, "Then who can be saved?" ²⁶But Jesus looked at them and said, "For mortals it is impossible, but for God all things are possible."*

*<sup>27</sup>Then Peter said in reply, "Look, we have left everything and followed you. What then will we have?" <sup>28</sup>Jesus said to them, "Truly I tell you, at the renewal of all things, when the Son of Man is seated on the throne of his glory, you who have followed me will also sit on twelve thrones, judging the twelve tribes of Israel. <sup>29</sup>And everyone who has left houses or brothers or sisters or father or mother or children or fields, for my name's sake, will receive a hundredfold, and will inherit eternal life. <sup>30</sup>But many who are first will be last, and the last will be first.*

Jesus continues to teach his followers about the cost of discipleship. Living in the reign of God affects not only one's most intimate relationships and life choices, but also one's use of money and anything that could stand in the way of following Jesus fully. Jesus' conversation with the wealthy young man is reminiscent of Micah 6:6–8, in which God's people ask three questions about what God requires of them. The prophet responds by stating God's three requirements for what is "good" for his people: "to do justice, and to love kindness, and to walk humbly with your God."

Here the young man asks three questions of Jesus, each of which is followed by Jesus' response, leading the man to a fuller understanding of what God requires of him. To the question about what good deed he must do to have eternal life, Jesus responds by shifting the man's focus from his own goodness to God's goodness (verse 17). The only way to seek the good is to follow God's will, the foundation of which is following the commandments of the Torah. To the young man's question concerning which commandments to obey, Jesus lists five of the ten commandments from Mount Sinai and the command to "love your neighbor as yourself" from Leviticus 19:18. Affirming that he has kept the commandments and nevertheless realizing that his response to God's will for his life is incomplete, he asks his last question, "What do I still lack?" (verse 20).

Jesus' final response gets to the main point of his instructions so that the young man may be "perfect" in his response to God (verse 21). The word translated "perfect" does not suggest flawlessness, but is better expressed as "whole" or "complete," a spiritual development that is deeper than simply following external commands. As Jesus tells the young man to sell his possessions, give them to the poor, and then follow him, he is attempting to move the man to the level of genuine discipleship. For entering God's kingdom is not just a matter of doing good deeds, but more importantly, taking away whatever obstacles prevent one from living completely under God's reign. For this young man, that obstacle is an acquisitiveness that has led him to have many possessions. He is unable to become a disciple because he is too attached to his wealth and is unable to rid himself of what prevents him from having a heart fully invested in God's kingdom.

Jesus' instructions to the wealthy young man are directed toward his own specific needs. All disciples must help the poor, but not all must divest themselves of possessions to do so. Yet, his interchange with the young man provides Jesus with an occasion to teach his disciples about the incompatibility of love for wealth and the kingdom. Jesus' unforgettable metaphor utilizes the largest animal of their experience, the camel, and the smallest opening, the needle's eye (verse 24). The astonishment of the disciples to Jesus' hyperbole enables Jesus to redirect their focus to God's initiative and power within them: "For God all things are possible."

Since it is impossible for human beings to save themselves and earn eternal life, does that make the efforts of the disciples pointless? Peter's question, "What then will we have?" and the response of Jesus assure the disciples that nothing they do with commitment to Jesus is in vain (verses 27–30). The twelve disciples will have glorious roles in the age to come. When the twelve tribes of Israel are gathered together again in the coming age, the twelve disciples will rule over this renewed people of God that Jesus is establishing. Even though now they seem to have given up everything, their losses will be made up many times over and they will experience the fullness of life forever. Even though now they seem poor and persecuted, seeming to be the "last" in the eyes of the world, they will be "first" as they share in God's glory.

## Reflection and Discussion

• Why was the wealthy young man unable to do what Jesus asked of him? Why did he go away grieving?

• Why did Jesus add the command, "Love your neighbor as yourself," for this young man? Had he followed this commandment?

• Why does Jesus use such a radical comparison to emphasize the incompatibility of wealth and discipleship? What reassurance and hope does Jesus give to those who are wealthy?

• How do possessions affect the disposition of my heart? Which possessions might be preventing me from following Jesus fully?

## Prayer

*Good Teacher, guide me as I continue to follow you and understand the costs of discipleship. Help me to know the obstacles that block you from fully entering my life. Free me from everything that keeps me from the experience of eternal life.*

# SUGGESTIONS FOR FACILITATORS, GROUP SESSION 2

1. If there are newcomers who were not present for the first group session, introduce them now.

2. You may want to pray this prayer as a group:

*Lord our God, enlightened by the glory of the Transfiguration and encouraged by the promises of eternal life, help us as we study Christ's teachings and follow his call to discipleship. As we are led by Jesus into the realm of the impossible, help us to trust in him and not fail in times of testing. May we unleash from our lives the obstacles of wealth, greed, pride, and everything that prevents us from following Jesus. May we forgive one another without limits, as you have forgiven us. Guide us to take up our crosses and accept the costs of discipleship.*

3. Ask one or more of the following questions:
   - What was your biggest challenge in Bible study over this past week?
   - What did you learn about yourself this week?

4. Discuss lessons 1 through 6 together. Assuming that group members have read the Scripture and commentary during the week, there is no need to read it aloud. As you review each lesson, you might want to briefly summarize the Scripture passages of each lesson and ask the group what stands out most clearly from the commentary.

5. Choose one or more of the questions for reflection and discussion from each lesson to talk over as a group. You may want to ask group members which question was most challenging or helpful to them as you review each lesson.

6. Keep the discussion moving, but don't rush the discussion in order to complete more questions. Allow time for the questions that provoke the most discussion.

7. Instruct group members to complete lessons 7 through 12 on their own during the six days before the next group meeting. They should write out their own answers to the questions as preparation for next week's group discussion.

8. Conclude by praying aloud together the prayer at the end of lesson 6, or any other prayer you choose.

"Friend, I am doing you no wrong; did you not agree with me
for the usual daily wage? Take what belongs to you and go;
I choose to give to this last the same as I give to you."

Matt 20:13–14

# Parable of the Vineyard Workers

**MATTHEW 20:1–16** ¹*"For the kingdom of heaven is like a landowner who went out early in the morning to hire laborers for his vineyard.* ²*After agreeing with the laborers for the usual daily wage, he sent them into his vineyard.* ³*When he went out about nine o'clock, he saw others standing idle in the marketplace;* ⁴*and he said to them, 'You also go into the vineyard, and I will pay you whatever is right.' So they went.* ⁵*When he went out again about noon and about three o'clock, he did the same.* ⁶*And about five o'clock he went out and found others standing around; and he said to them, 'Why are you standing here idle all day?'* ⁷*They said to him, 'Because no one has hired us.' He said to them, 'You also go into the vineyard.'* ⁸*When evening came, the owner of the vineyard said to his manager, 'Call the laborers and give them their pay, beginning with the last and then going to the first.'* ⁹*When those hired about five o'clock came, each of them received the usual daily wage.* ¹⁰*Now when the first came, they thought they would receive more; but each of them also received the usual daily wage.* ¹¹*And when they received it, they grumbled against the landowner,* ¹²*saying, 'These last worked only one hour, and you have made them equal to us who have borne the* *burden of the day and the scorching heat.' *[13]*But he replied to one of them, 'Friend, I am doing you no wrong; did you not agree with me for the usual daily wage? *[14]*Take what belongs to you and go; I choose to give to this last the same as I give to you. *[15]*Am I not allowed to do what I choose with what belongs to me? Or are you envious because I am generous?' *[16]*So the last will be first, and the first will be last."*

The parable expands the puzzling statement of Jesus, "The last will be first, and the first will be last" (verse 16). The first part of the parable describes the hiring of the laborers—from first to last (verses 1–7). The second part describes the payment of the laborers—from the last to the first (verses 8–15). This structure of the parable enhances the message of reversal in Jesus' mysterious maxim.

The parable opens with the familiar introduction, "The kingdom of heaven is like…" The vineyard owner hires workers at various periods throughout the day, from sunup to sundown. Though it is not directly stated, we can assume it is harvest time since the owner hires day laborers in the marketplace due to the urgency of completing the work on time. After the owner assures those hired early in the morning of the usual day's wage, those hired later are promised a just payment. Presumably this recompense will be proportionately less than the full day's wage. Toward the end of the day, the owner returns to the marketplace and finds others waiting for work. When he asks them why they are idle, they reply that no one has hired them. It seems that all who are willing to work are finally hired to work in the vineyard.

When the owner instructs his manager to pay the workers at the end of the day, they are paid "beginning with the last and then going to the first." Those hired last must have been astonished to receive the full daily wage. As those who were hired first and worked all day in the vineyard watch this, they expect to receive much more. When they are paid the same daily wage as the others, they grumble against the landowner, stating that the payment seems unfair.

The owner of the vineyard replies graciously but decisively. The laborers received exactly what was agreed. The landowner is free to do what he wishes with what belongs to him. For reasons known only to the owner, he desires to be especially generous to the last group of workers. So the parable ends not on the usual assumptions about what constitutes a fair wage, but on the sovereignty and generosity of the vineyard owner. He is the one who determines that the last will be first and the first will be last.

Like many parables of the gospel, this one is open to many levels of interpretation. The vineyard is a traditional symbol for Israel, a symbolism most prominent in the parable of Isaiah 5:1–7. The vineyard owner represents God, who graciously rewards his people in the judgment at the end of the age. For Jesus' listeners, the parable expresses the reality that God's generosity vastly exceeds human merit-based expectations. Disciples who have sacrificed a long time in the service of God's kingdom must not grumble about how God chooses to reward others. Those who follow God's commands closely are warned not to despise the outcasts such as tax collectors and sinners. The parable's stress on the equality of all before God would have been a pointed lesson for the Jewish Christians addressed by Matthew's gospel. They were the ones who had persevered in the vineyard of Israel with much labor, yet they should not be jealous of God's lavish generosity toward the latecomers, the Gentiles and sinners gathered into the kingdom by Jesus.

## Reflection and Discussion

• How do I feel about the laborers who worked twelve hours receiving the same wage as those hired an hour before quitting time?

• To which group of laborers do I belong in this parable? What is the message of the parable for me?

• Is the landowner's practice unjust or generous, or both? Why?

• How does this parable expound the teaching of Jesus that "the last will be first, and the first will be last"?

• When have I been jealous of the good fortunes of another? How frequently do I recognize the undeserved blessings of my life?

## Prayer

*Merciful Lord, when I compare myself to others, I often become jealous and resentful. Help me to keep focused on your goodness to me and give me a grateful heart. Thank you for calling me to labor in the vineyard of your kingdom.*

**"Whoever wishes to be great among you must be your servant, and whoever wishes to be first among you must be your slave."**

Matt 20:26–27

# To Drink the Cup

**MATTHEW 20:17–34** *17 While Jesus was going up to Jerusalem, he took the twelve disciples aside by themselves, and said to them on the way, 18 "See, we are going up to Jerusalem, and the Son of Man will be handed over to the chief priests and scribes, and they will condemn him to death; 19 then they will hand him over to the Gentiles to be mocked and flogged and crucified; and on the third day he will be raised."*

*20 Then the mother of the sons of Zebedee came to him with her sons, and kneeling before him, she asked a favor of him. 21 And he said to her, "What do you want?" She said to him, "Declare that these two sons of mine will sit, one at your right hand and one at your left, in your kingdom." 22 But Jesus answered, "You do not know what you are asking. Are you able to drink the cup that I am about to drink?" They said to him, "We are able." 23 He said to them, "You will indeed drink my cup, but to sit at my right hand and at my left, this is not mine to grant, but it is for those for whom it has been prepared by my Father."*

*24 When the ten heard it, they were angry with the two brothers. 25 But Jesus called them to him and said, "You know that the rulers of the Gentiles lord it over them, and their great ones are tyrants over them. 26 It will not be so among you; but whoever wishes to be great among you must be your servant, 27 and whoever wishes to be first among you must be your slave; 28 just as the Son of*

35

*Man came not to be served but to serve, and to give his life a ransom for many."*

[29]*As they were leaving Jericho, a large crowd followed him.* [30]*There were two blind men sitting by the roadside. When they heard that Jesus was passing by, they shouted, "Lord, have mercy on us, Son of David!"* [31]*The crowd sternly ordered them to be quiet; but they shouted even more loudly, "Have mercy on us, Lord, Son of David!"* [32]*Jesus stood still and called them, saying, "What do you want me to do for you?"* [33]*They said to him, "Lord, let our eyes be opened."* [34]*Moved with compassion, Jesus touched their eyes. Immediately they regained their sight and followed him.*

As Jesus is traveling with his disciples toward Jerusalem, he gives the longest and most detailed prediction of his passion and death. Each component—being handed over to the religious authorities, condemned to death, handed over to the Gentiles, mocked, flogged, crucified, and then raised on the third day—forms a section of the upcoming passion account of the gospel. The two-part handing over of Jesus, to the Jewish leaders and then to the Roman authorities, stresses the universality of his rejection. This prediction mentions the specific sufferings of Jesus including crucifixion, which is a Roman means of execution, not a Jewish mode of punishment.

Shockingly juxtaposed to Jesus' description of his coming suffering is the bold request of the mother of James and John. She asks Jesus to give her two sons the top positions of honor in his kingdom, "one at your right hand and one at your left" (verse 21). Evidently the disciples had prompted their mother's request since Jesus responds directly to James and John. None of them seem to understand the significance of his passion predictions or the nature of his kingdom. Jesus' response focuses on the image of drinking the cup, a metaphor used by the prophets to refer to Israel's suffering (verse 22). Jesus applies the image to his approaching passion, promising James and John that they too will eventually share in his suffering. Jesus wants them to concentrate on whether or not they can accept the cross, rather than on any prestige, status, or power.

Jesus sees in this presumptuous request a teaching moment for his disciples. He contrasts the oppressive and tyrannical power inflicted by Roman authorities on their subjects with the ministry that must characterize his church (verse 25). Those who wish to be great must be the servants; those who wish to be first must be the slaves. Jesus explains that the purpose of his ministry is service of others, and the purpose of his death is to ransom them from the captivity of sin. Seeking honors and domineering power is a gross misunderstanding of God's kingdom. The humble service and redemptive suffering of Jesus are the values of God's reign which Jesus calls his disciples to share.

As Jesus travels the last stage of his journey to Jerusalem, two blind men are sitting by the side of the road. Knowing that Jesus is the messianic healer, they call out to him, "Have mercy on us, Son of David!" (verse 30). The humble plea of the two blind men contrasts with the audacious request of the two disciples. When asked by Jesus what they desire, their response is an unassuming prayer: "Lord, let our eyes be opened" (verse 33). Their trust in Jesus stands out against the blindness of the disciples who do not see his redeeming power or understand the kingdom he is inaugurating. The healing of the two men's blindness results in their determination to follow Jesus on the road to Jerusalem.

## Reflection and Discussion

• In what ways does the attraction of prestige and power hamper the mission of Christ's church today?

• How does the plea of the two blind men contrast to the blind request of the two disciples?

• How do I answer the question of Jesus, "What do you want me to do for you?" (verse 32)? Is my answer more like that of the disciples or like that of the blind men?

• What does Jesus mean by his question, "Are you able to drink the cup?" (verse 22)? In what ways do I drink the cup of Jesus (verse 23)?

• How can I transform the energy of my status-seeking into a desire to give myself in service?

## Prayer

*Lord of the kingdom, your cross is your royal throne and those to your right and left are the servants and slaves of your people. Thank you for ransoming me from the captivity of sin so that I can reign with you.*

"Hosanna to the Son of David!
Blessed is the one who comes in the name of the Lord!
Hosanna in the highest heaven!"
Matt 21:9

# The Son of David Enters Jerusalem

**MATTHEW 21:1–11** ¹*When they had come near Jerusalem and had reached Bethphage, at the Mount of Olives, Jesus sent two disciples, ²saying to them, "Go into the village ahead of you, and immediately you will find a donkey tied, and a colt with her; untie them and bring them to me. ³If anyone says anything to you, just say this, 'The Lord needs them.' And he will send them immediately." ⁴This took place to fulfill what had been spoken through the prophet, saying,*

⁵*"Tell the daughter of Zion,*
*Look, your king is coming to you,*
*humble, and mounted on a donkey,*
*and on a colt, the foal of a donkey."*

⁶*The disciples went and did as Jesus had directed them; ⁷they brought the donkey and the colt, and put their cloaks on them, and he sat on them. ⁸A very large crowd spread their cloaks on the road, and others cut branches from the trees and spread them on the road. ⁹The crowds that went ahead of him and that followed were shouting,*

*"Hosanna to the Son of David!*

   *Blessed is the one who comes in the name of the Lord!*

*Hosanna in the highest heaven!"*

[10]*When he entered Jerusalem, the whole city was in turmoil, asking, "Who is this?"* [11]*The crowds were saying, "This is the prophet Jesus from Nazareth in Galilee."*

Jesus and his disciples have at last reached the destination of their travels from Galilee. The upward hike from the Jordan Valley and the town of Jericho has brought them to the Mount of Olives, just east of Jerusalem. From here the view of Jerusalem across the valley to the west is magnificent. Though Jesus could have slipped into the city undetected under cover of darkness, he made careful plans for his entry in fulfillment of the Scriptures. The crowds of pilgrims streaming to Jerusalem to celebrate the feast of Passover enhanced his triumphal entrance into David's city.

Jesus' entry into Jerusalem is a visual teaching and an enacted parable of the upside-down values of the kingdom. The familiar scene of a conquering king parading gloriously into a city is transformed into a scene which embodies the humble dignity that typifies God's kingdom. The king is dressed not in royal splendor or military trappings but in the simple dress of a Jewish teacher. He is meek and humble, not bellicose and splendorous. He rides not a mighty war-horse, but a young donkey. Jesus' royal authority is clearly in view as he triumphantly approaches the majestic city and its stately temple. Yet, this is a king like no other. The mixed signals perplex the citizens and pilgrims of the city.

As he enters Jerusalem, Jesus acts out the prophecy of Zechariah in order to dramatize the kind of Messiah he is. He has instructed his disciples to bring the donkey and its colt so that he may enter Jerusalem in the manner described by the prophet. Zechariah had announced a king riding into Jerusalem, "triumphant and victorious," yet "humble and mounted on a donkey." (Zech 9:9–10). This royal ruler for whom the people rejoice and shout for joy is further described by the prophet as banishing the implements of war and commanding "peace to the nations."

The residents of the city and the pilgrims who have come for the feast spread their cloaks along the road and place branches from the trees to carpet the way, literally giving him the royal treatment. They shout, "Hosanna to the

Son of David," a cry of praise hailing Jesus as David's Son, the Messiah. The acclamation from Psalm 118:25–26 continues with the shout, "Blessed is the one who comes in the name of the Lord!" (This psalm was prayed at Passover and sung as pilgrims entered the holy city.) The people of Jerusalem are accustomed to crowds of high-spirited pilgrims entering the city for the feasts, but when Jesus makes his entrance, "the whole city [is] in turmoil." People are asking about the identity of the one who enters with such a flourish.

The gospel confronts its readers with the same question: "Who is this?" The crowd replies to the people of Jerusalem, "This is the prophet Jesus from Nazareth in Galilee." Their answer is accurate but inadequate. The question "Who is this?" hovers over the remainder of the gospel during Jesus' last days. Each section of Jesus' final days in Jerusalem presents a partial answer to this critical question.

## Reflection and Discussion

• What might Jesus have wished the crowds to understand about him by the way he entered Jerusalem?

• In what sense is the crowd's identification of Jesus accurate but inadequate? What might be left to understand about Jesus as the gospel continues?

## Prayer

*Son of David, the city trembled and acknowledged you as the one who comes in the name of the Lord. Enter into my life today and reign as my King and Lord. Hosanna in the highest heaven!*

"Truly I tell you, if you have faith and do not doubt, not only will you do what has been done to the fig tree, but even if you say to this mountain, 'Be lifted up and thrown into the sea,' it will be done."

Matt 21:21

# Confrontation in the Temple

**MATTHEW 21:12–22** ¹²*Then Jesus entered the temple and drove out all who were selling and buying in the temple, and he overturned the tables of the money changers and the seats of those who sold doves.* ¹³*He said to them, "It is written,*

'*My house shall be called a house of prayer*';

*but you are making it a den of robbers.*"

¹⁴*The blind and the lame came to him in the temple, and he cured them.* ¹⁵*But when the chief priests and the scribes saw the amazing things that he did, and heard the children crying out in the temple, "Hosanna to the Son of David," they became angry* ¹⁶*and said to him, "Do you hear what these are saying?" Jesus said to them, "Yes; have you never read,*

'*Out of the mouths of infants and nursing babies*

*you have prepared praise for yourself*'?"

¹⁷*He left them, went out of the city to Bethany, and spent the night there.*

¹⁸*In the morning, when he returned to the city, he was hungry.* ¹⁹*And seeing a fig tree by the side of the road, he went to it and found nothing at all on it but leaves. Then he said to it, "May no fruit ever come from you again!" And the fig*

*tree withered at once.* [20]*When the disciples saw it, they were amazed, saying, "How did the fig tree wither at once?"* [21]*Jesus answered them, "Truly I tell you, if you have faith and do not doubt, not only will you do what has been done to the fig tree, but even if you say to this mountain, 'Be lifted up and thrown into the sea,' it will be done.* [22]*Whatever you ask for in prayer with faith, you will receive."*

After entering the city of Jerusalem, Jesus goes immediately to the colonnaded precincts of the temple. There he performs another visual teaching, like his royal entry into the city. In the temple courtyard he performs two prophetic actions: He clears the holy grounds of corrupt financial dealings and he removes the barriers preventing the disabled from participating in temple sacrifices. In this way, Jesus again manifests the upside-down values of God's kingdom, right in the heart of Israel's life. In clearing the temple, Jesus casts out the insiders; in healing the outcasts, he brings in the outsiders.

The commercial activity taking place on the grounds of the temple centered on the sacrificial system. The temple tax could be paid only in approved currency, so the money changers exchanged Greek and Roman coins with their pagan images for the coins suitable for temple offerings. Others were selling doves, the permissible sacrifice for those who could not afford to offer a lamb. Jesus' revulsion was not against the financial activities in themselves, since these transactions were necessary for fulfilling the requirements of the Torah. The offense to Jesus was evidently that these commercial dealings were happening within the sacred precincts of the temple and probably because the merchants were dealing deceitfully with the pilgrims. Other banks and markets were available in the city, but the high priest had recently set up this activity in the temple area to enrich the priestly families.

Jesus bases his disruptive and cleansing actions on biblical passages demonstrating the incompatibility of turning God's "house of prayer" into "a den of robbers" (verse 13). Isaiah had proclaimed that the temple would be a "house of prayer for all peoples," where sacrifices would be acceptable to God (Isa 56:7). Jeremiah had declared that, because the temple had become "a den of robbers," it would be destroyed (Jer 7:1–15). In this prophetic action, by disrupting the buying and selling connected with sacrificial worship in the temple, Jesus foreshadows the end of temple sacrifice and the destruction of God's house.

Jesus' healing of "the blind and the lame" has particular significance within the locale of the temple (verse 14). In the account of David's capture of Jerusalem, there is a mysterious reference to the blind and the lame (2 Sam 5:8). Becoming blind and lame was possibly part of a curse that would befall invaders if they dared to enter the city. For some reason, David had a fearful hatred for these disabled persons and they were later systematically expelled from the temple. By healing the blind and the lame, Jesus not only restores them physically but also removes the barrier to their full participation in God's house of prayer. Now even the children are singing out in praise of this "Son of David" (verse 15). All of these ways of renewing the temple—purifying it of corruption and opening it for the worship of all God's people—anger the chief priests and religious leaders and begin the process that will lead to Jesus' arrest.

Jesus performs one more symbolic action when he returns to the city the next morning (verse 18). His cursing of the fig tree because it bore no fruit expresses another judgment upon the temple and Jerusalem's religious leaders. The withered tree is a sign of the barren faith of Israel's leaders and of the temple's fate because of their failures. With the fig tree as a visual aid, Jesus urges his disciples to have strong faith, the faith that moves mountains. If "this mountain" refers to the mount on which the temple is built, its being thrown into the sea may be another image of the temple's pending destruction. These three symbolic actions—riding the donkey into the city, purifying the temple, and withering the fig tree—all express Jesus' royal and prophetic role in contrast to the ways in which the present religious leaders have misguided the legacy of ancient Israel. Jesus contrasts their barrenness with the potential fruitfulness of his disciples if they have faith in him.

## Reflection and Discussion

• If Jesus were to visit my church, work, or home, where might he begin overturning tables?

• In what ways did Jesus' actions in the temple demonstrate the upside-down values of God's kingdom?

• Why did Jesus disrupt the commercial activities in the temple if they were a necessary service for pilgrims?

• What does the dramatized parable of the fig tree teach me about faith and discipleship?

## Prayer

*Lord of the temple, you desire the holy sanctuary to be a house of prayer for all God's people. Deepen my faith in you so that when you come to me, you will find me bearing fruit for the kingdom.*

> "Truly I tell you, the tax collectors and the prostitutes
> are going into the kingdom of God ahead of you."
>
> Matt 21:31

# Questions about True Authority

**MATTHEW 21:23–32** ²³*When he entered the temple, the chief priests and the elders of the people came to him as he was teaching, and said, "By what authority are you doing these things, and who gave you this authority?"* ²⁴*Jesus said to them, "I will also ask you one question; if you tell me the answer, then I will also tell you by what authority I do these things.* ²⁵*Did the baptism of John come from heaven, or was it of human origin?" And they argued with one another, "If we say, 'From heaven,' he will say to us, 'Why then did you not believe him?'* ²⁶*But if we say, 'Of human origin,' we are afraid of the crowd; for all regard John as a prophet."* ²⁷*So they answered Jesus, "We do not know." And he said to them, "Neither will I tell you by what authority I am doing these things.*

²⁸*"What do you think? A man had two sons; he went to the first and said, 'Son, go and work in the vineyard today.'* ²⁹*He answered, 'I will not'; but later he changed his mind and went.* ³⁰*The father went to the second and said the same; and he answered, 'I go, sir'; but he did not go.* ³¹*Which of the two did the will of his father?" They said, "The first." Jesus said to them, "Truly I tell you, the tax collectors and the prostitutes are going into the kingdom of God ahead of you.* ³²*For John came to you in the way of righteousness and you did not believe him,*

*but the tax collectors and the prostitutes believed him; and even after you saw it, you did not change your minds and believe him."*

Then Jesus returns to the temple, his controversy with the religious leaders continues in earnest. This running debate gets more and more impassioned as it continues over the next several chapters and leads to the passion account. The ongoing series of challenges to Jesus flows from this single question: "By what authority are you doing these things, and who gave you this authority?" The focus remains on Jesus' authority, a fundamental issue of Matthew's gospel, an authority that is acknowledged by the Jewish crowds but rejected by the Jewish leaders.

Jesus responds to the questions of the Jewish leaders with a counter-question, thereby creating a dilemma for his opponents. If they admit that John the Baptist's authority came "from heaven," they will expose their own unbelief, but if they say it was "of human origin," they will anger the crowds who believe that both John and Jesus are prophets from God. Caught in the quandary with their insincerity exposed, the leaders choose to plead ignorance. Their admission of ignorance proves that they are incompetent to pronounce judgment on the deeds of Jesus. Though Jesus, in turn, refuses to answer their question about the source of his authority, the readers of the gospel have no doubt about the answer.

In the parable of the two sons, the sons respond oppositely to their father's request that they work in his vineyard. The first son refuses at first, but later he changes his mind and goes. The second son says that he will go, but in fact he does not go to work in the vineyard. This time, the opponents of Jesus answer his question, stating that the son who did the father's will was the one who actually worked in the vineyard. Yet by this answer they denounce themselves, since they are the ones who say yes to God in words but disobey in deeds.

As Jesus applies the message of the parable, he states that "the tax collectors and the prostitutes" are entering the kingdom ahead of the religious leaders. The sinners who repent are like the first son because they actually work in the vineyard despite their initial refusal. The religious leaders, on the other hand, are like the second son because they promise to work but they actually do nothing. Even though they claim to do God's will and even have heard the preaching of John the Baptist, they refuse to repent and demonstrate an obedient faith.

The parable teaches that discipleship is fundamentally about what one does, not just about what one says. Some may claim in words to be religious, but their lack of deeds and lack of genuine repentance and obedient faith betray their hypocrisy. Yet amazingly, the grace of God shown in repentance can draw even notorious sinners into the kingdom. The kingdom is promised not to those who merely say "I will go," but to those who actually do the will of the Father.

## Reflection and Discussion

• How does the answer of the religious leaders, "We do not know," prove their inability to judge the teachings and deeds of Jesus?

• What similar teachings are made by the enacted parable of the fig tree without fruit and the parable of the two sons?

• Do I walk the way I talk? What is the lesson of the parable for disciples today?

## Prayer

*Good Teacher, you desire to draw all people into the kingdom through the divine authority of your teachings. Do not allow my words to remain idle but help me to do your Father's will by putting them into practice in my life.*

"Therefore I tell you, the kingdom of God
will be taken away from you and given to a people that
produces the fruits of the kingdom."
Matt 21:43

# Parable of the Deceitful Tenants

**MATTHEW 21:33–46** [33]*"Listen to another parable. There was a landowner who planted a vineyard, put a fence around it, dug a wine press in it, and built a watchtower. Then he leased it to tenants and went to another country.* [34]*When the harvest time had come, he sent his slaves to the tenants to collect his produce.* [35]*But the tenants seized his slaves and beat one, killed another, and stoned another.* [36]*Again he sent other slaves, more than the first; and they treated them in the same way.* [37]*Finally he sent his son to them, saying, 'They will respect my son.'* [38]*But when the tenants saw the son, they said to themselves, 'This is the heir; come, let us kill him and get his inheritance.'* [39]*So they seized him, threw him out of the vineyard, and killed him.* [40]*Now when the owner of the vineyard comes, what will he do to those tenants?"* [41]*They said to him, "He will put those wretches to a miserable death, and lease the vineyard to other tenants who will give him the produce at the harvest time."*

[42]*Jesus said to them, "Have you never read in the scriptures:*
*'The stone that the builders rejected*
*has become the cornerstone;*

*this was the Lord's doing,*
   *and it is amazing in our eyes'?*
[43]*Therefore I tell you, the kingdom of God will be taken away from you and given to a people that produces the fruits of the kingdom.* [44]*The one who falls on this stone will be broken to pieces; and it will crush anyone on whom it falls."*

[45]*When the chief priests and the Pharisees heard his parables, they realized that he was speaking about them.* [46]*They wanted to arrest him, but they feared the crowds, because they regarded him as a prophet.*

The parable is an allegory of God's saving history with his people. The images are rooted in the prophecy of Isaiah, in which Israel is described as God's vineyard. God demonstrates his loving care for the vineyard by preparing the ground, planting the vines, building a watchtower, and hewing out a winepress (Isa 5:1–2). In the parable of Jesus, the owner leases the vineyard to tenant farmers while he is away on a journey. These tenants are contractually obliged to produce a harvest for the owner of the vineyard. This entire description reflects the traditional grape-growing practices of the region.

The owner of the vineyard is God, while the tenants are Israel's leaders who were charged to care for God's people through the centuries. The critical question of the plot concerns how the owner will receive his share of the harvest. The owner's slaves, sent to collect the harvest, are the prophets of Israel who have been mistreated and put to death through the centuries by the leaders of the people. When the owner finally sends his own son to collect the harvest, the tenants reason that they will acquire the vineyard for themselves if they can do away with the owner's heir. Of course, the son is Jesus himself as he is confronted by the religious leaders of his day. The parable situates Jesus within the line of Israel's rejected prophets, yet also affirms his unique status as the Father's Son and heir. The parable dramatizes the son's fate: "They seized him, threw him out of the vineyard, and killed him" (verse 39)—details that anticipate the death of Jesus outside the walls of Jerusalem.

Jesus draws his listeners into the story by asking the religious leaders to finish the parable: "Now when the owner of the vineyard comes, what will he do to those tenants?" (verse 40). Jesus' listeners realize that the owner's incredible patience is at an end, and so they reply that the owner will destroy those tenants for their wickedness and give over the vineyard to new tenants who will give the owner his share of the harvest. As in the previous parable, the religious leaders denounce themselves with their answer.

Jesus then verifies the self-incriminating answer of Israel's leaders by quoting from Psalm 118, again confirming the gospel's fundamental conviction that Jesus' messianic ministry fulfills the ancient Scriptures. In moving from the parable to the psalm, Jesus switches from agricultural to architectural imagery: "The stone that the builders rejected has become the cornerstone." In Hebrew, the word for "stone" and the word for "son" are similar, creating a wordplay. The son put to death by the tenants is the rejected stone which becomes the most important stone of the new structure. Jesus, who was rejected and put to death, will become the foundation of God's church when God raises him from the dead.

As Jesus applies his teaching, he declares that the kingdom of God will be taken away from the religious leaders and given to those who will produce "the fruits of the kingdom" (verse 43). A common interpretation of this parable suggests that the kingdom is taken away from Israel and given to the church. Yet, it is not the vineyard that is replaced; it is the tenants. God does not replace his people with a different people; he replaces the leadership of Israel with the disciples of Jesus. Peter and the other Jewish disciples will be given leadership over those who are entering the kingdom of God. They will be expected to produce fruit within God's vineyard and deliver the harvest for God.

This application of the parable is confirmed as the chief priests and the Pharisees realize that Jesus is speaking about them (verse 45). God will replace those who have failed to lead his people rightly with those who will. It is this community of Jews faithful to the covenant of Israel, led by the Jewish disciples of Jesus, who will become the nucleus of the emerging church.

## Reflection and Discussion

• If I were an absent owner and entrusted my property to others, what qualities would I look for in tenants? What qualities need to be present in those who lead the community of Jesus' disciples?

• Who are the tenants in this allegory? In what way does the parable portray God's ongoing care for Israel?

• Why don't the religious leaders arrest Jesus after hearing his parable? Why don't they repent and follow him?

• In what ways could this parable be applicable to the leaders of God's people today?

## Prayer

*Jesus, you are the heir of your Father's vineyard and the Lord of God's people. May the leaders of your church listen to your teaching so that they may guide your disciples to produce a rich harvest for God's kingdom.*

# SUGGESTIONS FOR FACILITATORS, GROUP SESSION 3

1. Welcome group members and ask if there are any announcements anyone would like to make.

2. You may want to pray this prayer as a group:

*Father of our Lord Jesus Christ, you have called us to labor in the vineyard of your kingdom. As your Son entered Jerusalem, he was welcomed by the crowds and threatened by those in power. Guide us as we follow Jesus and listen to the teachings of his parables. Form us as faithful disciples and free us from the obstacles that stand in the way of our service. Deepen our faith and give us grateful hearts. Continue calling us into the vineyard so that we may produce a rich harvest for your kingdom where Jesus is King and Lord.*

3. Ask one or more of the following questions:
   • Which image from the lessons this week stands out most memorably to you?
   • What is the most important lesson you learned through your study this week?

4. Discuss lessons 7 through 12. Choose one or more of the questions for reflection and discussion from each lesson to discuss as a group. You may want to ask group members which question was most challenging or helpful to them as you review each lesson.

5. Remember that there are no definitive answers for these discussion questions. The insights of group members will add to the understanding of all. None of these questions require an expert.

6. After talking about each lesson, instruct group members to complete lessons 13 through 18 on their own during the six days before the next group meeting. They should write out their own answers to the questions as preparation for next week's group discussion.

7. Ask the group if anyone is having any particular problems with the Bible study during the week. You may want to share advice and encouragement within the group.

8. Conclude by praying aloud together the prayer at the end of one of the lessons discussed. You may add to the prayer based on the sharing that has occurred in the group.

**"Those slaves went out into the streets and gathered all whom they found, both good and bad; so the wedding hall was filled with guests."** Matt 22:10

# Parable of the Wedding Feast

**MATTHEW 22:1–14** *¹Once more Jesus spoke to them in parables, saying: ²"The kingdom of heaven may be compared to a king who gave a wedding banquet for his son. ³He sent his slaves to call those who had been invited to the wedding banquet, but they would not come. ⁴Again he sent other slaves, saying, 'Tell those who have been invited: Look, I have prepared my dinner, my oxen and my fat calves have been slaughtered, and everything is ready; come to the wedding banquet.' ⁵But they made light of it and went away, one to his farm, another to his business, ⁶while the rest seized his slaves, mistreated them, and killed them. ⁷The king was enraged. He sent his troops, destroyed those murderers, and burned their city. ⁸Then he said to his slaves, 'The wedding is ready, but those invited were not worthy. ⁹Go therefore into the main streets, and invite everyone you find to the wedding banquet.' ¹⁰Those slaves went out into the streets and gathered all whom they found, both good and bad; so the wedding hall was filled with guests.*

*¹¹"But when the king came in to see the guests, he noticed a man there who was not wearing a wedding robe, ¹²and he said to him, 'Friend, how did you get in here without a wedding robe?' And he was speechless. ¹³Then the king said to* *the attendants, 'Bind him hand and foot, and throw him into the outer darkness, where there will be weeping and gnashing of teeth.' *[14]*For many are called, but few are chosen."*

A s Jesus continues his encounter with the religious leaders of Jerusalem, he tells another parable. As is typical in Matthew's gospel, the parable illustrates an aspect of God's kingdom. The story tells of a king who gives a royal wedding feast for his son. When the time arrives, the king sends out his slaves to call those who have been previously invited to come to the banquet. The first call is rejected and the invited guests refuse to come. So the king sends out a second set of slaves with the urgent call, "Everything is ready, come to the wedding banquet" (verse 4). Some merely brush the invitation aside and go on their way; others seize the slaves, mistreat them, and put them to death. In response, the king sends in troops, destroys the murderers, and burns their city (verse 7).

As in the previous parable of the deceitful tenants and the vineyard, we see the father-son relationship and varying responses to the request of the slaves. The reader understands that the king is God and the king's son is Jesus. Again, the parable shows that the defiance of Israel's leaders toward God's messengers is consistent throughout history. The urgent call of the slaves that the banquet is ready expresses the nearness of the kingdom. The range of responses to the slaves' call, from indifference to violent hostility, portrays the varying responses of Israel to the call of John the Baptist and Jesus. The king's angry response to his disloyal subjects represents God's judgment of the religious establishment in Jerusalem. The destruction of Jerusalem and the burning of its temple come at the hands of the Romans, just as the Hebrew Scriptures had attributed Assyria, Babylon, and Persia as the instruments of God's judgment.

When the king sends out his servants for the final time, he instructs them to invite everyone they find to the wedding banquet (verse 9). As the slaves do as they are told, the wedding hall is filled with a new set of invitees. If the originally invited guests represent the religious establishment of Jerusalem, the newly invited guests are the emerging church composed of Jews and Gentiles who respond in faith to the Messiah.

The parable notes that the hall is filled with guests who are "both good and bad" (verse 10). When the king comes to greet his guests, he notices that one is not wearing proper attire for the wedding (verse 11). Since the man cannot explain his insulting attire, he is arrested, cast out of the dining hall, and punished. This final element of the parable expresses the truth that the church is a mixed reality, consisting of wheat and weeds, good and bad. The wedding robe that the guest fails to wear represents the deeds of repentance that must accompany one admitted to God's kingdom. While God invites everyone, only those who do the will of the Father will enter the kingdom of heaven (see 7:21). The criteria for authentic discipleship remain the same for the people of Israel and for the Gentiles. One cannot be complacent about God's reign, but must remain faithful and responsive to the call.

## Reflection and Discussion

• Why would Jesus represent God's kingdom as a royal wedding banquet? What can make people indifferent to God's invitation to the kingdom? Why do I sometimes feel unresponsive to my invitation to Christ's royal feast?

• What is the meaning of the king inviting everyone to the wedding banquet? What are the implications of God gathering the undeserving to the feast?

## Prayer

*Royal Son of God, the feast is prepared and all people are called to the wedding. May I respond with heartfelt gratitude to the invitation and put on the garment of faithful service. Welcome me to the banquet of the kingdom.*

"You shall love the Lord your God with all your heart,
and with all your soul, and with all your mind."
This is the greatest and first commandment. Matt 22:37

# Controversial Questions in the Temple Area

**MATTHEW 22:15–46** ¹⁵*Then the Pharisees went and plotted to entrap him in what he said.* ¹⁶*So they sent their disciples to him, along with the Herodians, saying, "Teacher, we know that you are sincere, and teach the way of God in accordance with truth, and show deference to no one; for you do not regard people with partiality.* ¹⁷*Tell us, then, what you think. Is it lawful to pay taxes to the emperor, or not?"* ¹⁸*But Jesus, aware of their malice, said, "Why are you putting me to the test, you hypocrites?* ¹⁹*Show me the coin used for the tax." And they brought him a denarius.* ²⁰*Then he said to them, "Whose head is this, and whose title?"* ²¹*They answered, "The emperor's." Then he said to them, "Give therefore to the emperor the things that are the emperor's, and to God the things that are God's."* ²²*When they heard this, they were amazed; and they left him and went away.*

²³*The same day some Sadducees came to him, saying there is no resurrection; and they asked him a question, saying,* ²⁴*"Teacher, Moses said, 'If a man dies childless, his brother shall marry the widow, and raise up children for his brother.'* ²⁵*Now there were seven brothers among us; the first married, and died childless, leaving the widow to his brother.* ²⁶*The second did the same, so also the third,*

down to the seventh. [27]*Last of all, the woman herself died.* [28]*In the resurrection, then, whose wife of the seven will she be? For all of them had married her."*

[29]*Jesus answered them, "You are wrong, because you know neither the scriptures nor the power of God.* [30]*For in the resurrection they neither marry nor are given in marriage, but are like angels in heaven.* [31]*And as for the resurrection of the dead, have you not read what was said to you by God,* [32]*'I am the God of Abraham, the God of Isaac, and the God of Jacob'? He is God not of the dead, but of the living."* [33]*And when the crowd heard it, they were astounded at his teaching.*

[34]*When the Pharisees heard that he had silenced the Sadducees, they gathered together,* [35]*and one of them, a lawyer, asked him a question to test him.* [36]*"Teacher, which commandment in the law is the greatest?"* [37]*He said to him, "'You shall love the Lord your God with all your heart, and with all your soul, and with all your mind.'* [38]*This is the greatest and first commandment.* [39]*And a second is like it: 'You shall love your neighbor as yourself.'* [40]*On these two commandments hang all the law and the prophets."*

[41]*Now while the Pharisees were gathered together, Jesus asked them this question:* [42]*"What do you think of the Messiah? Whose son is he?" They said to him, "The son of David."* [43]*He said to them, "How is it then that David by the Spirit calls him Lord, saying,*

[44]*'The Lord said to my Lord,*

*"Sit at my right hand,*

*until I put your enemies under your feet"'?*

[45]*If David thus calls him Lord, how can he be his son?"* [46]*No one was able to give him an answer, nor from that day did anyone dare to ask him any more questions.*

Jesus' conflict with the leaders in Jerusalem continues with four additional controversies: taxes to Caesar, the resurrection, the greatest commandment, and David's Son. Each of these disputes begins with a question. Three of these questions are presented by the religious leaders, the Pharisees, Sadducees, and Herodians, and Jesus successfully answers them, one by one, to the amazement of his opponents and the crowds. The final question comes from Jesus himself and concerns the identity of the Messiah. When his opponents are unable to answer his one question, the controversies end and no one dares to ask Jesus any more questions.

The first question is clearly intended to entrap Jesus. If Jesus supports paying taxes to the emperor without qualification, he will alienate the Pharisees and seem too compliant for those who resent the Roman occupation. If Jesus rejects paying the tax, he will alienate the Herodians who depend on Roman favor and he will put himself in the dangerous situation of repudiating Roman authority. Jesus is aware of the malice behind their flattering words and fabricated smiles, so he asks to see one of the coins. With this visual aid, Jesus shows them the bust of Tiberius Caesar on the coin with the words in Latin, "Tiberius Caesar, august son of the Divine High Priest Augustus." When his opponents admit that the image and inscription on the coin is that of the emperor, Jesus says, "Give therefore to the emperor the things that are the emperor's, and to God the things that are God's" (verse 21). Neither the image of Caesar nor its blasphemous inscription belongs in God's temple, and it seems appropriate to pay it back to the emperor. Jesus' reply teaches that allegiance to God supersedes allegiance to Rome and its emperor. He startles his interrogators with his wisdom and sends them away confounded.

The second question is again intended to discredit Jesus and also to demonstrate the supposed absurdity of the resurrection. The complicated case is based on the Torah's teaching on levirate marriage which obligates a man to marry his brother's widow in order to provide her with children. In the hypothetical situation posed by the Sadducees, a woman was married to seven brothers in succession, each of whom died childless. They ask Jesus to which of her husbands she will be married in the resurrection. Rather than answering the question directly, Jesus tells his interrogators that they know "neither the Scriptures nor the power of God" (verse 29). They do not understand God's power to transform human existence because people, like angels, do not live as married couples in the resurrection. They do not understand the Scriptures because God's words to Moses from the burning bush confirm that God's covenant with Abraham, Isaac, and Jacob did not end with their death but implies their resurrection. The Sadducees can produce no response to Jesus and the watching crowd is astounded.

The third and final attempt to entrap Jesus comes as a lawyer asks Jesus a test question. Utterly respectful of Israel's Torah, Jesus states that two texts sum up all the commandments. The first is from Deuteronomy 6:5, the creed of Israel, instructing absolute love for God. The second is from Leviticus 19:18, teaching love for God's human creatures. Jesus states that all Scripture, the law and the prophets of Israel, is an exposition of the ideals expressed in these two commands. As Jesus has shown throughout his teachings, the law of love is the guiding principle for interpreting all of Scripture.

After responding wisely to the three questions of his opponents, Jesus turns the tables and questions them. The key question concerns the Messiah: "Whose son is he?" (verse 42). While the response of the Pharisees that the Messiah is "the son of David" is correct, it does not adequately describe the full identity of Jesus. Jesus then asks how David himself, under the inspiration of the Spirit, calls the Messiah "my Lord" in Psalm 110. With the religious leaders unable to answer him, Jesus has silenced all his opponents. The question is left hanging, to be answered by the disciples and readers of the gospel. Jesus is indeed the Son of David, but he is also David's Lord and the beloved Son of God.

## Reflection and Discussion

• How does Jesus transcend the "either-or" question about whether it is lawful or not to pay taxes to the emperor? What is the point Jesus is making?

• In what way does my belief in the God of Abraham, Isaac, and Jacob help my belief in the resurrection? What further strengthens my belief?

## Prayer

*Lord of David and Son of God, you teach me that my primary obligation is not to human authority but to God. As I seek to love God with my whole being and to love God's people, help me to root my interpretation of Scripture on these two commands.*

"Do whatever they teach you and follow it;
but do not do as they do, for they do not practice
what they teach." Matt 23:3

# Warning Disciples Against Hypocrisy

**MATTHEW 23:1–12** ¹*Then Jesus said to the crowds and to his disciples,*
²*"The scribes and the Pharisees sit on Moses' seat; ³therefore, do whatever they
teach you and follow it; but do not do as they do, for they do not practice what
they teach. ⁴They tie up heavy burdens, hard to bear, and lay them on the shoulders of others; but they themselves are unwilling to lift a finger to move them.
⁵They do all their deeds to be seen by others; for they make their phylacteries
broad and their fringes long. ⁶They love to have the place of honor at banquets
and the best seats in the synagogues, ⁷and to be greeted with respect in the mar-
ketplaces, and to have people call them rabbi. ⁸But you are not to be called rabbi,
for you have one teacher, and you are all students. ⁹And call no one your father
on earth, for you have one Father—the one in heaven. ¹⁰Nor are you to be called
instructors, for you have one instructor, the Messiah. ¹¹The greatest among you
will be your servant. ¹²All who exalt themselves will be humbled, and all who
humble themselves will be exalted."*

J esus culminates his running dispute with the leaders of Jerusalem's religious establishment with these indictments. Yet the various religious leaders are no longer present, and Jesus speaks only to "the crowds" and his disciples." Jesus' bitter denunciation of the scribes and Pharisees is aimed at the community who will form his church. It is a sober warning not to follow in their ways.

Jesus first acknowledges that these Jewish authorities are to be respected for their role as the official teachers of the Torah. The early followers of Jesus did not turn their backs on their Jewish heritage or the leaders of the synagogues. Yet, Jesus warns his followers not to imitate these authorities, "for they do not practice what they teach" (verse 3). Though Jesus shared many of the concerns of these teachers, he points out several ways that their example is inconsistent with their teaching and must not be imitated.

Jesus states that the official teachers lay heavy burdens on people's shoulders by their insistence on meticulous observance of the Sabbath and ritual washings, but they make no effort to lighten the load or help people carry the burden (verse 4). They are preoccupied with relatively trivial matters while neglecting the internal qualities that animate obedience to the Torah. Jesus also points out the inconsistency of the Jewish authorities because "they do all their deeds to be seen by others" (verse 5). Jesus then illustrates this general statement with six examples, arranged in three pairs. First, they widen their phylacteries, small leather containers with the words of the Torah attached to the arm and forehead. Second, they lengthen their fringes, the tassels worn on the lower hem of cloaks as reminders to keep God's commandments. Third, they seek the place of honor at banquets, the most prestigious seats next to the host. Fourth, they covet the best seats in the synagogues, the prominent places where they can be seen.

Fifth, they want to be greeted with titles of respect in the marketplace; and sixth, they are preoccupied with honorific designations like rabbi. It would be a mistake to assume that all religious officials in Jerusalem shared these qualities. Rather, Jesus chooses several examples of haughty behavior that he cautions his disciples not to replicate.

Jesus then forbids the ostentatious use of honorific titles among his disciples. Any pretentious greetings, like "rabbi," "father," or "instructor," that express a relationship of status and power are inappropriate for his followers (verses 8–10). Humility, not arrogance, should characterize discipleship. True greatness pertains to service, not privilege. A servant does not lay heavy burdens on the shoulders of others, but bears their burdens. A servant does not seek attention, because a servant's attention is on the needs of others. A servant is not concerned about prestige, for a servant claims no titles. A servant simply serves, and within the community of disciples that is true greatness.

## Reflection and Discussion

• Why is it so difficult to respect leaders who do not practice what they teach? In what ways does my walk sometimes fail to express my talk?

• Lusting for honors and praise is a temptation that can beset all disciples in every aspect of life. How does this distorted desire limit the effectiveness of life in family, business, and church?

• What are some of the distinctive characteristics Jesus wishes for the community of his disciples?

## Prayer

*Jesus, you are the one teacher of your church, and you instruct your disciples to practice what we teach. Help me to be a humble servant within your church and show me the way to simply serve, unconcerned with attention, prestige, and honors.*

"Jerusalem, Jerusalem, the city that kills the prophets
and stones those who are sent to it! How often have I desired to gather
your children together as a hen gathers her brood under her wings."

Matt 23:37

# Woes Against the Religious Leaders

**MATTHEW 23:13–39** [13] *"But woe to you, scribes and Pharisees, hypocrites! For you lock people out of the kingdom of heaven. For you do not go in yourselves, and when others are going in, you stop them.* [15] *Woe to you, scribes and Pharisees, hypocrites! For you cross sea and land to make a single convert, and you make the new convert twice as much a child of hell as yourselves.*

[16] *"Woe to you, blind guides, who say, 'Whoever swears by the sanctuary is bound by nothing, but whoever swears by the gold of the sanctuary is bound by the oath.'* [17] *You blind fools! For which is greater, the gold or the sanctuary that has made the gold sacred?* [18] *And you say, 'Whoever swears by the altar is bound by nothing, but whoever swears by the gift that is on the altar is bound by the oath.'* [19] *How blind you are! For which is greater, the gift or the altar that makes the gift sacred?* [20] *So whoever swears by the altar, swears by it and by everything on it;* [21] *and whoever swears by the sanctuary, swears by it and by the one who dwells in it;* [22] *and whoever swears by heaven, swears by the throne of God and by the one who is seated upon it.*

<sup>23</sup>*"Woe to you, scribes and Pharisees, hypocrites! For you tithe mint, dill, and cummin, and have neglected the weightier matters of the law: justice and mercy and faith. It is these you ought to have practiced without neglecting the others.* <sup>24</sup>*You blind guides! You strain out a gnat but swallow a camel!*

<sup>25</sup>*"Woe to you, scribes and Pharisees, hypocrites! For you clean the outside of the cup and of the plate, but inside they are full of greed and self-indulgence.* <sup>26</sup>*You blind Pharisee! First clean the inside of the cup, so that the outside also may become clean.*

<sup>27</sup>*"Woe to you, scribes and Pharisees, hypocrites! For you are like whitewashed tombs, which on the outside look beautiful, but inside they are full of the bones of the dead and of all kinds of filth.* <sup>28</sup>*So you also on the outside look righteous to others, but inside you are full of hypocrisy and lawlessness.*

<sup>29</sup>*"Woe to you, scribes and Pharisees, hypocrites! For you build the tombs of the prophets and decorate the graves of the righteous,* <sup>30</sup>*and you say, 'If we had lived in the days of our ancestors, we would not have taken part with them in shedding the blood of the prophets.'* <sup>31</sup>*Thus you testify against yourselves that you are descendants of those who murdered the prophets.* <sup>32</sup>*Fill up, then, the measure of your ancestors.* <sup>33</sup>*You snakes, you brood of vipers! How can you escape being sentenced to hell?* <sup>34</sup>*Therefore I send you prophets, sages, and scribes, some of whom you will kill and crucify, and some you will flog in your synagogues and pursue from town to town,* <sup>35</sup>*so that upon you may come all the righteous blood shed on earth, from the blood of righteous Abel to the blood of Zechariah son of Barachiah, whom you murdered between the sanctuary and the altar.* <sup>36</sup>*Truly I tell you, all this will come upon this generation.*

<sup>37</sup>*"Jerusalem, Jerusalem, the city that kills the prophets and stones those who are sent to it! How often have I desired to gather your children together as a hen gathers her brood under her wings, and you were not willing!* <sup>38</sup>*See, your house is left to you, desolate.* <sup>39</sup>*For I tell you, you will not see me again until you say, 'Blessed is the one who comes in the name of the Lord.'"*

Jesus' woes against Jerusalem's religious leaders must be understood against the background of the biblical prophets who frequently denounced the sins of Israel's leaders with alarm and justifiable anger. The woe oracles developed from the covenant curses, which dramatically expressed the terrible price Israel would pay for its violation of the covenant with God (see the twelve curses in Deut 27:15–26). His severe language had a familiar ring, and the lament over Jerusalem at the end of the woes demonstrates that his words come from his own grief as much as from anger. Like the prophets, Jesus' relentless oracles are ultimately intended to turn a group of his own people from evil and to warn his disciples not to follow their practices.

In the series of woes, the scribes and Pharisees are repeatedly called "hypocrites," a term that originally referred to an actor on a stage who puts on a mask to pretend to be someone he is not. Jesus charges them with honoring God outwardly while their hearts are far from him, or saying one thing and doing another. Here Jesus selects certain practices that he found in the religion of his own day which express the insincerity and lack of integrity that can creep into any religious institution when its prophetic voice is silenced.

The seven woes are pronounced in three pairs followed by a final climactic woe. The first pair accuses the leaders of preventing people from entering God's kingdom and leading them astray (verses 13–15). In contrast, disciples must shepherd the flock with vigilance and carefully seek out the stray. The next pair of woes charges Jesus' opponents with scrupulously attending to the minute matters of the law while neglecting the central values that support religious practices (verses 16–24). Jesus' examples about taking oaths and tithing demonstrate how the hypocritical authorities neglect the weightier matters of justice, mercy, and faith. The third pair of woes rebukes the tendency of religious leaders to focus on external issues to the detriment of internal matters (verses 25–28). The metaphors of washing tableware and of whitewashed tombs express how the exterior can be clean and beautiful, while the interior is full of filth and greed. In contrast, Jesus teaches what is at the core of Israel's Torah: Obedience to God's law must emanate from the heart.

The seventh and final woe accuses the present-day religious authorities of being no different from their ancestors who murdered the prophets (verses 29–32). The crucifixion of Jesus will be the culmination of this historical pattern of rejecting the ones sent by God, beginning with Abel and continuing through Zechariah, the first and last victims of murder in the Hebrew Bible (verse 35). Jesus also portends the persecution of his disciples at the hands of these same authorities, and he declares God's judgment on those who are guilty. His words certainly do not indict the Jewish people as a whole; rather the harsh rhetoric is that of a Jewish teacher speaking to and within his own people.

The harsh accusations give way to heart-rending grief as Jesus expresses his tender desire for the people of Jerusalem (verse 37). His primary emotion is compassion as he laments their fate with unspeakable sadness. Despite the opposition of many of Jerusalem's leaders and the terrible suffering ahead, Jesus is deeply moved for his people and for the beautiful city and its temple. The image of the hen and her chicks speaks of Jesus' unrelenting solidarity with his people, not rejection. Though this scene marks the end of Jesus' public ministry in Jerusalem, his final words express the prophetic hope that the city will someday welcome him with joyful shouts as the One who comes in the name of the Lord.

## Reflection and Discussion

• Why is it so much easier to see the faults of others than to see my own mistakes in these seven woes? Which of these woes could justifiably incriminate me?

• What convinces me that Jesus is implicating the leaders of his church rather than Judaism itself in this address to his disciples?

## Prayer

*Messiah of Israel, you are the one who comes in the name of the Lord. Like the religious authorities of Jerusalem, I often put on the mask of piety when my heart is bitter and fail to live what I say I believe. Help me to seek justice, mercy, and faith.*

"He will send out his angels with a loud trumpet call,
and they will gather his elect from the four winds,
from one end of heaven to the other." Matt 24:31

# The Beginning of the End Time

**MATTHEW 24:1–35** ¹As Jesus came out of the temple and was going away, his disciples came to point out to him the buildings of the temple. ²Then he asked them, "You see all these, do you not? Truly I tell you, not one stone will be left here upon another; all will be thrown down."

³*When he was sitting on the Mount of Olives, the disciples came to him privately, saying, "Tell us, when will this be, and what will be the sign of your coming and of the end of the age?"*

⁴*Jesus answered them, "Beware that no one leads you astray. ⁵For many will come in my name, saying, 'I am the Messiah!' and they will lead many astray. ⁶And you will hear of wars and rumors of wars; see that you are not alarmed; for this must take place, but the end is not yet. ⁷For nation will rise against nation, and kingdom against kingdom, and there will be famines and earthquakes in various places: ⁸all this is but the beginning of the birthpangs.*

⁹*"Then they will hand you over to be tortured and will put you to death, and you will be hated by all nations because of my name. ¹⁰Then many will fall away, and they will betray one another and hate one another. ¹¹And many false prophets will arise and lead many astray. ¹²And because of the increase of lawlessness,*

the love of many will grow cold. ¹³*But the one who endures to the end will be saved.* ¹⁴*And this good news of the kingdom will be proclaimed throughout the world, as a testimony to all the nations; and then the end will come.*

¹⁵*"So when you see the desolating sacrilege standing in the holy place, as was spoken of by the prophet Daniel (let the reader understand),* ¹⁶*then those in Judea must flee to the mountains;* ¹⁷*the one on the housetop must not go down to take what is in the house;* ¹⁸*the one in the field must not turn back to get a coat.* ¹⁹*Woe to those who are pregnant and to those who are nursing infants in those days!* ²⁰*Pray that your flight may not be in winter or on a sabbath.* ²¹*For at that time there will be great suffering, such as has not been from the beginning of the world until now, no, and never will be.* ²²*And if those days had not been cut short, no one would be saved; but for the sake of the elect those days will be cut short.* ²³*Then if anyone says to you, 'Look! Here is the Messiah!' or 'There he is!' —do not believe it.* ²⁴*For false messiahs and false prophets will appear and produce great signs and omens, to lead astray, if possible, even the elect.* ²⁵*Take note, I have told you beforehand.* ²⁶*So, if they say to you, 'Look! He is in the wilderness,' do not go out. If they say, 'Look! He is in the inner rooms,' do not believe it.* ²⁷*For as the lightning comes from the east and flashes as far as the west, so will be the coming of the Son of Man.* ²⁸*Wherever the corpse is, there the vultures will gather.*

²⁹*"Immediately after the suffering of those days*
*the sun will be darkened,*
*and the moon will not give its light;*
*the stars will fall from heaven,*
*and the powers of heaven will be shaken.*
³⁰*Then the sign of the Son of Man will appear in heaven, and then all the tribes of the earth will mourn, and they will see 'the Son of Man coming on the clouds of heaven' with power and great glory.* ³¹*And he will send out his angels with a loud trumpet call, and they will gather his elect from the four winds, from one end of heaven to the other.*

³²*"From the fig tree learn its lesson: as soon as its branch becomes tender and puts forth its leaves, you know that summer is near.* ³³*So also, when you see all these things, you know that he is near, at the very gates.* ³⁴*Truly I tell you, this generation will not pass away until all these things have taken place.* ³⁵*Heaven and earth will pass away, but my words will not pass away."*

Following his conflicts with the various religious leaders of Jerusalem, Jesus leaves the temple for the last time. As he walks eastward across the Kidron Valley and toward the Mount of Olives, the disciples draw his attention to the magnificence of the temple. In response, Jesus speaks about its pending destruction: "Not one stone will be left here upon another" (verse 2). When he reaches the Mount of Olives, Jesus sits down and begins the fifth and final discourse of the gospel, the sermon on the last things (Matt 24–25).

The discourse is spoken privately to the disciples and in reply to their two-part question: When will the temple be destroyed and "what will be the sign of your coming and of the end of the age" (verse 3)? The response of Jesus makes it clear that the destruction of the temple and the final "coming" of the Messiah are two different events. For Matthew's community, the demolition of Jerusalem and its temple has already taken place and the coming of the end is an event to be expected in the future. Though for Jewish Christians the catastrophe of the Roman invasion of Jerusalem may seem like the end, the sermon on the last things makes it clear that this destruction is only a foreshadowing of "the end of the age" and the glorious "coming of the Son of Man."

The discourse begins by summarizing the many calamities the church will face throughout its existence. False messiahs will lead many astray and wars, devastating famines, and earthquakes will bring much fear. The church will face opposition from within and from without. Disciples will sufferer persecution, torture, and death from those who hate them, and many will fall away from their commitment to Jesus and betray their fellow disciples. Although in almost every age people see these kinds of disasters and wonder if they announce the end of the world, Jesus tells his disciples that these events are but "the beginning of the birth pangs" (verse 8). If such sufferings are not signs of the end but rather labor pains, then disciples can look forward in hope to the birth of something that will more than make up for the pain.

The mark of true discipleship in the midst of all these disasters is perseverance: "Anyone who endures to the end will be saved" (verse 13). This fidelity to Jesus will result in the message of the kingdom being proclaimed to the whole world (verse 14). Only when the full scope of this universal mission is completed will the travails end and the Son of Man return. From the perspective of Matthew's community, the end is not imminent because of the considerable mission the church has been given to bring the gospel to all the nations.

Jesus' discourse continues as he speaks more specifically of the Roman invasion of Jerusalem and the destruction of the temple. He likens these calamities to the "desolating sacrilege standing in the holy place," as prophesied by Daniel (verse 15). When these events occur, those in the area around Jerusalem must immediately flee to the mountains for refuge. As in most disasters, mothers and children are most severely affected. Disciples should pray that it does not happen in winter, when the rains make travel difficult, or on the Sabbath, when travel is restricted for Jews. As terrible as these events will be, they are only the foretaste of future events.

The coming of the Son of Man will be marked by unmistakable signs, and it will be as evident as lightening streaking across the sky or vultures circling over their prey (verses 27–28). The sermon weaves together several prophetic texts describing cosmic chaos: the darkening of the sun and moon, the stars falling from heaven, and the shaking of heaven's powers (verse 29). The "sign of the Son of Man" is imagery from the prophet Daniel. This glorious Son of Man, "coming with the clouds of heaven," will receive "dominion and glory and kingship, that all peoples, nations, and languages should serve him" (Dan 7:13–14).

The budding of the fig tree in the springtime is a clear sign that the fruit of summer is near. Similarly, "all these things" are signs that the coming of the Son of Man is "near" (verse 32–33). Even "this generation," the lifetime of those who hear the words of Jesus, will experience these signs, including the temple's destruction, which foretell the coming of Jesus in glory. As with most prophecy, these words of Jesus are capable of multiple fulfillments. These signs manifest themselves in every generation, portending the end of the age.

## Reflection and Discussion

• Which of the calamitous signs predicted by Jesus are the church and the world experiencing today?

• How does my understanding of these signs, as "the beginning of the birth pangs," offer me hope for the future?

• What is the task of the church today in light of Jesus' sermon on the last things? What is my role in this mission?

• What endures when all else passes away (verse 35)? In what can I place my firm trust (Isa 40:8)?

## Prayer

*Glorious Son of Man, you will come on the clouds of heaven with power and glory. Help me to persevere in the midst of trials and tribulations, and help me to proclaim the good news of the kingdom in anticipation of your return.*

"If the owner of the house had known in what part of the night the thief was coming, he would have stayed awake and would not have let his house be broken into." Matt 24:43

# Exhortation to Watchful Expectation

MATTHEW 24:36–51 *³⁶"But about that day and hour no one knows, neither the angels of heaven, nor the Son, but only the Father. ³⁷For as the days of Noah were, so will be the coming of the Son of Man. ³⁸For as in those days before the flood they were eating and drinking, marrying and giving in marriage, until the day Noah entered the ark, ³⁹and they knew nothing until the flood came and swept them all away, so too will be the coming of the Son of Man. ⁴⁰Then two will be in the field; one will be taken and one will be left. ⁴¹Two women will be grinding meal together; one will be taken and one will be left. ⁴²Keep awake therefore, for you do not know on what day your Lord is coming. ⁴³But understand this: if the owner of the house had known in what part of the night the thief was coming, he would have stayed awake and would not have let his house be broken into. ⁴⁴Therefore you also must be ready, for the Son of Man is coming at an unexpected hour.*

*⁴⁵"Who then is the faithful and wise slave, whom his master has put in charge of his household, to give the other slaves their allowance of food at the proper time? ⁴⁶Blessed is that slave whom his master will find at work when he arrives. ⁴⁷Truly I tell you, he will put that one in charge of all his possessions. ⁴⁸But if that wicked slave says to himself, 'My master is delayed,'* [49]*and he begins to beat his fellow slaves, and eats and drinks with drunkards,* [50]*the master of that slave will come on a day when he does not expect him and at an hour that he does not know.* [51]*He will cut him in pieces and put him with the hypocrites, where there will be weeping and gnashing of teeth."*

A s Jesus continues his sermon on the end times, he moves from a description of his future coming to a discussion of the relevance of his coming to present-day discipleship. A true understanding of Jesus' teachings about the end of the age must have a profound effect upon the way God's people live from day to day. The sermon is far more than mere prediction; it is an exhortation to alertness, faithfulness, and service.

The signs that Jesus has offered are imprecise and cannot be used to determine when Jesus will return in glory. Jesus insists that no one except the Father can know the day or the hour (verse 36). Though Jesus had the foresight of a prophet and a unique relationship with the Father, his human condition prevented him from knowing everything that is in the mind of God. Jesus compares the unpredictability of the end times with the days of Noah. The coming of the Son of Man will be as definitive and sudden as the flood. As people are working in the fields or grinding at the mill, many will be caught unaware (verses 40–41). Some will be taken into the kingdom of heaven; others will be left out of the kingdom in the darkness outside.

Jesus' teachings about alertness, faithfulness, and service are illustrated by brief parables. The story of the thief breaking into the house in the middle of the night underlines the fact that disciples do not know the timing of the Lord's coming. Jesus exhorts his disciples to "keep awake" and to "be ready" because "the Son of Man is coming at an unexpected hour" (verse 44).

The parable of the faithful and the wicked slaves contrasts the one who remains ready and the one who is caught unprepared. The faithful slave is put in charge of his master's household during his absence and is found doing his master's work when he returns (verse 46). This faithful slave is promoted and put in charge of all his master's possessions. In contrast, the wicked slave presumes that the master's return is a long way off and neglects his responsibilities. When his master unexpectedly returns and finds him recklessly disregarding his tasks, the wicked slave is subjected to a severe judgment.

The vivid imagery of Jesus' teaching urges his disciples to live in light of the future. Though the time of his coming is unknowable, the fact of his glorious return is certain. The church's ignorance of the time of the coming of the Son of Man should result in its constant watchfulness. Disciples must not take up an indifferent way of life. They must always be about their master's business, doing the work of the kingdom, vigilantly awaiting his coming in glory.

## Reflection and Discussion

• What part of Jesus' teachings indicates this sermon is more about the present than the future?

• Why is it foolish and dangerous to speculate about the time of the future coming of Christ?

• How am I preparing in a practical way for the glorious coming of the Lord?

## Prayer

*Saving Lord, we wait in joyful hope for your coming in glory. You teach us to always be ready though we cannot know the day of your coming. Keep me watchful and prepared, so that I will be found serving the needs of your kingdom when you return.*

# SUGGESTIONS FOR FACILITATORS, GROUP SESSION 4

1. Welcome group members and ask if anyone has any questions, announcements, or requests.

2. You may want to pray this prayer as a group:

*God of all people, in the temple of Jerusalem your Messiah taught the people of Israel. Through his parables and wisdom, may we learn how to love you with all our being and to love your people. With your word at the center of our lives, make us humble servants in your household, seeking justice and mercy rather than attention and honors. May we be found working as stewards of your kingdom when Jesus Christ comes with power and glory to establish your reign forever.*

3. Ask one or more of the following questions:
   - What is the most difficult part of this study for you?
   - What insights stand out to you from the lessons this week?

4. Discuss lessons 13 through 18. Choose one or more of the questions for reflection and discussion from each lesson to discuss as a group. You may want to ask group members which question was most challenging or helpful to them as you review each lesson.

5. Keep the discussion moving, but allow time for the questions that provoke the most discussion. Encourage the group members to use "I" language in their responses.

6. After talking over each lesson, instruct group members to complete lessons 19 through 24 on their own during the six days before the next group meeting. They should write out their own answers to the questions as preparation for next week's session.

7. Ask the group what encouragement they need for the coming week. Ask the members to pray for the needs of one another during the week.

8. Conclude by praying aloud together the prayer at the end of one of the lessons discussed. You may choose to conclude the prayer by asking members to pray aloud any requests they may have.

"The bridegroom came, and those who were ready
went with him into the wedding banquet."
Matt 25:10

# Parable of the Wise and Foolish Maidens

**MATTHEW 25:1–13** [1]*"Then the kingdom of heaven will be like this. Ten bridesmaids took their lamps and went to meet the bridegroom.* [2]*Five of them were foolish, and five were wise.* [3]*When the foolish took their lamps, they took no oil with them;* [4]*but the wise took flasks of oil with their lamps.* [5]*As the bridegroom was delayed, all of them became drowsy and slept.* [6]*But at midnight there was a shout, 'Look! Here is the bridegroom! Come out to meet him.'* [7]*Then all those bridesmaids got up and trimmed their lamps.* [8]*The foolish said to the wise, 'Give us some of your oil, for our lamps are going out.'* [9]*But the wise replied, 'No! there will not be enough for you and for us; you had better go to the dealers and buy some for yourselves.'* [10]*And while they went to buy it, the bridegroom came, and those who were ready went with him into the wedding banquet; and the door was shut.* [11]*Later the other bridesmaids came also, saying, 'Lord, lord, open to us.'* [12]*But he replied, 'Truly I tell you, I do not know you.'* [13]*Keep awake therefore, for you know neither the day nor the hour."*

In order to instruct his disciples on his future coming, Jesus again tells a parable. As in many of his previous teachings, the parable illustrates an aspect of the kingdom and begins with the words, "The kingdom of heaven will be like this." Through parables, Jesus both surprises and disturbs his listeners, jarring their presuppositions and moving them to new understandings. In order to unfold the mystery of the kingdom, which will be established in its fullness when the Son of Man comes in glory, the parable presents the coming Lord as the bridegroom. Similarly, the prophets had presented God as the bridegroom of Israel and expressed the covenant bond between God and his people through the imagery of marital love.

In the weddings of Jesus' day, the wedding party would accompany the bridegroom from the house of the bride to his own house, where the feasting would begin. The focus of the parable is on the ten bridesmaids who await the groom. Five of them are foolish because they expected the groom to arrive immediately and they did not bring extra oil for their lamps. The other five are wise because they anticipated that the groom might be delayed and they brought flasks of oil to replenish their lamps.

The bridegroom's delay in coming causes all the bridesmaids to get drowsy and fall asleep. When the announcement is made that the bridegroom's arrival is imminent, the wise maidens replenish their lamps with the oil while the foolish ones must go to the dealer to purchase more oil. At the coming of the bridegroom, the wise ones enter with him into the wedding banquet, but the foolish ones are shut out.

Jesus' conclusion to the parable emphasizes its lesson: Constant alertness is necessary because it is impossible to pinpoint the time of the Lord's coming. The parable is a warning to the church, which consists of both wise and foolish disciples. Matthew's gospel highlights this parable because, for the church of Matthew, the return of Jesus has indeed been delayed. Jesus has not returned as swiftly as many in the early church anticipated. The church must learn to remain vigilant, anticipating the Lord's coming while its members persevere in faithful service and proclaim the kingdom to the nations.

## Reflection and Discussion

• Why do Jesus and the prophets use the symbolism of marriage to express the covenant between God and his people?

• What is the oil that I must keep in steady supply in order to be ready to meet the Lord when he comes again?

• Why is watchfulness such an important quality of the Christian life? How can I remain vigilant?

## Prayer

*Jesus the Bridegroom, you urge us to await your coming with watchful anticipation and joyful hope. Show me how to keep the lamps of my discipleship burning brightly so that I can keep vigil for your coming and celebrate your arrival when you come in glory.*

"Well done, good and trustworthy slave; you have been trustworthy
in a few things, I will put you in charge of many things;
enter into the joy of your master." Matt 25:21

# Parable on Investing Talents

MATTHEW 25:14–30 ¹⁴"For it is as if a man, going on a journey, summoned his slaves and entrusted his property to them; ¹⁵to one he gave five talents, to another two, to another one, to each according to his ability. Then he
went away. ¹⁶The one who had received the five talents went off at once and
traded with them, and made five more talents. ¹⁷In the same way, the one who
had the two talents made two more talents. ¹⁸But the one who had received the
one talent went off and dug a hole in the ground and hid his master's money.
¹⁹After a long time the master of those slaves came and settled accounts with
them. ²⁰Then the one who had received the five talents came forward, bringing
five more talents, saying, 'Master, you handed over to me five talents; see, I have
made five more talents.' ²¹His master said to him, 'Well done, good and trustworthy slave; you have been trustworthy in a few things, I will put you in charge
of many things; enter into the joy of your master.' ²²And the one with the two
talents also came forward, saying, 'Master, you handed over to me two talents;
see, I have made two more talents.' ²³His master said to him, 'Well done, good
and trustworthy slave; you have been trustworthy in a few things, I will put you
in charge of many things; enter into the joy of your master.' ²⁴Then the one who
had received the one talent also came forward, saying, 'Master, I knew that you
were a harsh man, reaping where you did not sow, and gathering where you did

*not scatter seed;* <sup>25</sup>*so I was afraid, and I went and hid your talent in the ground. Here you have what is yours.'* <sup>26</sup>*But his master replied, 'You wicked and lazy slave! You knew, did you, that I reap where I did not sow, and gather where I did not scatter?* <sup>27</sup>*Then you ought to have invested my money with the bankers, and on my return I would have received what was my own with interest.* <sup>28</sup>*So take the talent from him, and give it to the one with the ten talents.* <sup>29</sup>*For to all those who have, more will be given, and they will have an abundance; but from those who have nothing, even what they have will be taken away.* <sup>30</sup>*As for this worthless slave, throw him into the outer darkness, where there will be weeping and gnashing of teeth.'"*

Jesus continues to instruct his disciples about what to do during the period between his departure and his glorious return. Again he offers a parable to express the importance of diligence and faithfulness while living in watchfulness. The issue in not when the master will return or whether the slaves will be surprised by his return but whether they are dependable in using the master's resources entrusted to them.

The parable has a clear structure. First, the master distributes his resources: five talents, two talents, and one talent. Next, the slaves express their stewardship: five talents are doubled, two talents are doubled, and one talent is hidden in the ground. Finally, the master offers recompense for their stewardship: reward for the first, reward for the second, and punishment for the third. Each slave is entrusted with a certain amount of money, determined according to the ability of each one (verse 15). The "talent" was originally a measure of weight, but here it denotes a large sum of money, so even the slave entrusted with only one talent was delegated a substantial responsibility. The industrious slaves do business with the resources and eventually increase their amount by 100 percent. The slave with one talent, however, buries it in the ground, a common practice in the ancient world for keeping valuables secure.

In this parable, Jesus is clearly the master whose departure and return frame the events in the story. The three slaves express different types of disciples who make up the church during the Lord's bodily absence. The large amount entrusted to each slave expresses the greatness of God's gifts to his people. The master is away for a considerably long time before returning to settle accounts (verse 19). But when he arrives, the judgment of the slaves is based on their stewardship of the master's resources. The first two slaves are described as "good and trustworthy," and the master rewards their faithfulness by giving them more responsibility.

The third slave attempts to persuade the master that the caution he exercised in burying his talent in the ground was commendable. He has returned what the master gave him in full. But the master calls him "wicked and lazy," and he takes the talent from him and gives it to the slave with the ten talents. Because he has earned nothing for his master, he is described as "worthless" and is deprived from entering his master's joy.

The question Jesus will ask when he returns is, "What have you been doing since I left you?" The task of discipleship is to use one's gifts to extend God's reign in the world. Inactivity is the result of fear and laziness. Such uselessness is incompatible with genuine discipleship.

Good stewardship of one's abilities and opportunities expresses faithfulness to Jesus as his disciples await his coming in glory. When Jesus returns he will call his disciples to account for that stewardship.

## Reflection and Discussion

• The English word "talent" is derived from this parable. What abilities, gifts, and talents am I putting to use in the service of Jesus?

• Why would the first two slaves receive the same reward, even though the first accomplished quantitatively more than the second?

• Why was the third slave punished so severely, even though he returned the full amount he was given by the master? What does his fate teach me about discipleship?

• If the purpose of the parable is to instruct the church about how to live between the departure of Jesus and his glorious return, what is its message for the church today?

• What advice might I offer to a person seeking ways to discern his or her life calling?

## Prayer

*Master and Lord, you have given me more than I could ever deserve, but I so often let your gifts go to waste. Show me how to use the talents and abilities you have given me for the sake of your kingdom.*

"Truly I tell you, just as you did it to one of the least of these
who are members of my family, you did it to me."

Matt 25:40

# The Judgment of All the Nations

**MATTHEW 25:31–46** ³¹"*When the Son of Man comes in his glory, and all the angels with him, then he will sit on the throne of his glory. ³²All the nations will be gathered before him, and he will separate people one from another as a shepherd separates the sheep from the goats, ³³and he will put the sheep at his right hand and the goats at the left. ³⁴Then the king will say to those at his right hand, 'Come, you that are blessed by my Father, inherit the kingdom prepared for you from the foundation of the world; ³⁵for I was hungry and you gave me food, I was thirsty and you gave me something to drink, I was a stranger and you welcomed me, ³⁶I was naked and you gave me clothing, I was sick and you took care of me, I was in prison and you visited me.' ³⁷Then the righteous will answer him, 'Lord, when was it that we saw you hungry and gave you food, or thirsty and gave you something to drink? ³⁸And when was it that we saw you a stranger and welcomed you, or naked and gave you clothing? ³⁹And when was it that we saw you sick or in prison and visited you?' ⁴⁰And the king will answer them, 'Truly I tell you, just as you did it to one of the least of these who are members of my family, you did it to me.' ⁴¹Then he will say to those at his left hand, 'You that are accursed, depart from me into the eternal fire prepared for* *the devil and his angels;* <sup>42</sup>*for I was hungry and you gave me no food, I was thirsty and you gave me nothing to drink,* <sup>43</sup>*I was a stranger and you did not welcome me, naked and you did not give me clothing, sick and in prison and you did not visit me.'* <sup>44</sup>*Then they also will answer, 'Lord, when was it that we saw you hungry or thirsty or a stranger or naked or sick or in prison, and did not take care of you?'* <sup>45</sup>*Then he will answer them, 'Truly I tell you, just as you did not do it to one of the least of these, you did not do it to me.'* <sup>46</sup>*And these will go away into eternal punishment, but the righteous into eternal life."*

Jesus' sermon on the last things ends climactically with this great judgment scene. The long discourse which began with the disciples' question about Jesus' coming at the end of the age concludes with his coming to judge all the nations. The other teachings of Jesus have urged alertness and faithfulness as the correct way to wait for his coming. This teaching on the last judgment adds compassion toward those in need as the appropriate way to live between the departure of Jesus and his glorious return.

Jesus describes himself as the glorious Son of Man who comes with all his angels and sits on his glorious throne. The scene is a universal gathering of "all the nations." This messianic King acts as a shepherd, a common metaphor for royal rulers, and separates people as a shepherd separates sheep from goats. The King determines who will enter his kingdom, seemingly using a single standard for making this judgment.

Those on the King's right are those who are blessed by the Father and inherit the kingdom prepared for them (verse 34). Jesus declares them blessed because they helped him when he was hungry, thirsty, away from home, naked, sick, and imprisoned. The blessed ones express puzzlement and ask when they saw Jesus in need and helped him. Apparently they can remember doing acts of compassion for others, but they can't remember doing such deeds for Jesus. Jesus responds that their acts of compassion were done for him whenever they did them for one of the least of his brothers or sisters.

Those on the King's left have committed an appalling sin of omission. Jesus declares that they turned their back on him when he was hungry, thirsty, away from home, naked, sick, and imprisoned. These are just as perplexed as those who are blessed. They apparently do not deny their refusal to come to the aid of those in need, but they do not recall refusing to serve Jesus in his need.

Jesus responds that their denial of help to one of the least of his brothers or sisters was a refusal to come to his aid.

Jesus repeats the mention of those who are hungry, thirsty, away from home, naked, sick, and imprisoned a total of four times in this scene. This repetition imprints these needy least ones on the minds of his listeners and certainly on the minds of those who listen to the gospel. No one reflecting on this account of the last judgment can have any doubt that Jesus wants his followers to show compassion to those in need. The concluding statement stresses the awesome nature of the choice: eternal punishment and eternal life. Jesus stresses the everlasting significance of the decision whether or not to help the least ones. The blessed will experience inexpressible joys in God's presence forever, and the accursed will experience unspeakable horror in separation from God.

Jesus' family is worldwide, and his brothers and sisters include all who are in need of life's basic necessities: food, drink, hospitality, clothing, health care, and companionship. He is the king of the whole world and the ultimate judge of all humanity. Yet he is about to allow himself to be handed over for trial, crucifixion, and death. With this scene of final judgment and the end of the age, Jesus has concluded all his teachings. The lessons that Jesus wishes his disciples to perpetuate and instill into the future followers in his church are complete.

## Reflection and Discussion

• What is the common element contained in all six actions mentioned by Jesus? What would be another action Jesus might mention today?

• In light of Jesus' portrayal of how I will be judged, what do I need to do that I am not doing?

• In light of Jesus' judgment of the nations, how might this teaching challenge my nation's policies on poverty, nutrition, health care, prisons, or immigration?

• What is the great surprise for both those on the right and the left of Jesus? In what way does this scene enforce the theme of Matthew's gospel that Jesus is always with his church?

## Prayer

*King of the world, you are the ultimate judge of all people. You have taught us that whatever we do for the least among your brothers and sisters, we do for you. Help me to see your presence in those who are hungry, thirsty, away from home, naked, sick, and imprisoned.*

> "Truly I tell you, wherever this good news is proclaimed in the whole world, what she has done will be told in remembrance of her."
>
> Matt 26:13

# Treacherous Plotting and Anointing for Death

**MATTHEW 26:1–25** ¹*When Jesus had finished saying all these things, he said to his disciples,* ²*"You know that after two days the Passover is coming, and the Son of Man will be handed over to be crucified."*

³*Then the chief priests and the elders of the people gathered in the palace of the high priest, who was called Caiaphas,* ⁴*and they conspired to arrest Jesus by stealth and kill him.* ⁵*But they said, "Not during the festival, or there may be a riot among the people."*

⁶*Now while Jesus was at Bethany in the house of Simon the leper,* ⁷*a woman came to him with an alabaster jar of very costly ointment, and she poured it on his head as he sat at the table.* ⁸*But when the disciples saw it, they were angry and said, "Why this waste?* ⁹*For this ointment could have been sold for a large sum, and the money given to the poor."* ¹⁰*But Jesus, aware of this, said to them, "Why do you trouble the woman? She has performed a good service for me.* ¹¹*For you always have the poor with you, but you will not always have me.* ¹²*By pouring this ointment on my body she has prepared me for burial.* ¹³*Truly I tell you, wherever this good news is proclaimed in the whole world, what she has done will be told in remembrance of her."*

¹⁴*Then one of the twelve, who was called Judas Iscariot, went to the chief priests* ¹⁵*and said, "What will you give me if I betray him to you?" They paid him thirty pieces of silver.* ¹⁶*And from that moment he began to look for an opportunity to betray him.*

¹⁷*On the first day of Unleavened Bread the disciples came to Jesus, saying, "Where do you want us to make the preparations for you to eat the Passover?"* ¹⁸*He said, "Go into the city to a certain man, and say to him, 'The Teacher says, My time is near; I will keep the Passover at your house with my disciples.'"* ¹⁹*So the disciples did as Jesus had directed them, and they prepared the Passover meal.*

²⁰*When it was evening, he took his place with the twelve;* ²¹*and while they were eating, he said, "Truly I tell you, one of you will betray me."* ²²*And they became greatly distressed and began to say to him one after another, "Surely not I, Lord?"* ²³*He answered, "The one who has dipped his hand into the bowl with me will betray me.* ²⁴*The Son of Man goes as it is written of him, but woe to that one by whom the Son of Man is betrayed! It would have been better for that one not to have been born."* ²⁵*Judas, who betrayed him, said, "Surely not I, Rabbi?" He replied, "You have said so."*

With Jesus' teaching ministry now complete, the passion narrative begins. The narrative notes that Jesus "had finished saying all these things," meaning that his fifth and final discourse has ended. This conclusive statement is reminiscent of the words of Moses in the fifth book of the Torah: "When Moses had finished reciting all these words to all Israel..." (Deut 32:45). Just as the book of Deuteronomy completes Moses' instruction of Israel and begins the account of his death on Mount Nebo, the gospel concludes Jesus' instructions and begins the narrative that leads to his death.

The passion narrative is placed within the context of Israel's annual Passover (verse 2). This pilgrimage feast celebrates Israel's deliverance from slavery and God's covenant with his people. At the same time, it anticipates God's future redemption and the complete salvation of his people. Jesus' death and resurrection will constitute the new covenant and the definitive Passover. The Son of Man who is about to be handed over for crucifixion is the same Son of Man who will come and sit on the throne of his glory. Though the religious leaders choose not to arrest Jesus during the feast because the multitude of pilgrims could easily start a riot, the prophetic words of Jesus assure us that Passover and his death will coincide.

In contrast to the treachery and betrayal that dominate the passion account, the scene of the anonymous woman who anoints Jesus with costly ointment stands out for its tender generosity (verse 7). Her action demonstrates her devotion to Jesus and a genuine insight into the uniqueness of the hour. Jesus interprets her action as a prophetic anointing in preparation for his burial. Jesus' response to the male disciples' feigned concern for the poor is not a fatalistic declaration that ending poverty is hopeless (verse 11). Rather, he states that while disciples will always have the occasion and responsibility to assist the poor, their opportunity to offer devoted kindness to Jesus is drawing to a close. Jesus' final comment binds the memory of this woman's loving service into the gospel account (verse 13). Wherever his story is told, her story will be part of it. The sweet smell of her ointment fills this beautiful scene and briefly overcomes the stench of deceit and hostility that permeates the passion account. Meanwhile, Judas Iscariot strikes a pathetic bargain and initiates his betrayal. The thirty pieces of silver, taken in self-centered greed, contrast to the expensive ointment, given in selfless love.

On the first day of Unleavened Bread, Jesus makes preparation for the feast of Passover, which begins at sundown. Announcing, "My time is near," he secures a room to commemorate the Passover with the traditional Seder Supper (verse 18). The sacred bond of friendship and covenant evoked through the meal underscores the tragedy of Judas' betrayal. As the disciples ask Jesus, one after another, "Surely not I, Lord," every reader of Matthew's gospel must ask the same question, realizing that such betrayal is possible for anyone.

## Reflection and Discussion

• How could Judas the disciple become Judas the betrayer? Why does Matthew report that the disciples at table asked "one after another, 'Surely not I, Lord'"?

• Why does the gospel recount these events in the context of Israel's Passover?

• How did Jesus respond when the disciples described his anointing as a "waste"? What is Jesus teaching through his response?

• Why will the story of the woman's anointing be told in remembrance of her whenever the Passover of Jesus is celebrated in remembrance of him?

## Prayer

*Son of Man, as the time of your death drew near, you desired to celebrate the Passover with your disciples. May my discipleship be remembered like that of the women who anointed you rather than like Judas who betrayed you.*

**Peter said to him, "Even though I must die with you, I will not deny you."
And so said all the disciples.** Matt 26:35

# The Last Supper and Prayer in Gethsemane

**MATTHEW 26:26–46** ²⁶*While they were eating, Jesus took a loaf of bread, and after blessing it he broke it, gave it to the disciples, and said, "Take, eat; this is my body." ²⁷Then he took a cup, and after giving thanks he gave it to them, saying, "Drink from it, all of you; ²⁸for this is my blood of the covenant, which is poured out for many for the forgiveness of sins. ²⁹I tell you, I will never again drink of this fruit of the vine until that day when I drink it new with you in my Father's kingdom."*

³⁰*When they had sung the hymn, they went out to the Mount of Olives.*

³¹*Then Jesus said to them, "You will all become deserters because of me this night; for it is written,*

*'I will strike the shepherd,*

*and the sheep of the flock will be scattered.'*

³²*But after I am raised up, I will go ahead of you to Galilee." ³³Peter said to him, "Though all become deserters because of you, I will never desert you." ³⁴Jesus said to him, "Truly I tell you, this very night, before the cock crows, you will deny me three times." ³⁵Peter said to him, "Even though I must die with you, I will not deny you." And so said all the disciples.*

*<sup>36</sup>Then Jesus went with them to a place called Gethsemane; and he said to his disciples, "Sit here while I go over there and pray." <sup>37</sup>He took with him Peter and the two sons of Zebedee, and began to be grieved and agitated. <sup>38</sup>Then he said to them, "I am deeply grieved, even to death; remain here, and stay awake with me." <sup>39</sup>And going a little farther, he threw himself on the ground and prayed, "My Father, if it is possible, let this cup pass from me; yet not what I want but what you want." <sup>40</sup>Then he came to the disciples and found them sleeping; and he said to Peter, "So, could you not stay awake with me one hour? <sup>41</sup>Stay awake and pray that you may not come into the time of trial; the spirit indeed is willing, but the flesh is weak." <sup>42</sup>Again he went away for the second time and prayed, "My Father, if this cannot pass unless I drink it, your will be done." <sup>43</sup>Again he came and found them sleeping, for their eyes were heavy. <sup>44</sup>So leaving them again, he went away and prayed for the third time, saying the same words. <sup>45</sup>Then he came to the disciples and said to them, "Are you still sleeping and taking your rest? See, the hour is at hand, and the Son of Man is betrayed into the hands of sinners. <sup>46</sup>Get up, let us be going. See, my betrayer is at hand."*

Matthew's account of the meal consists of ritual words and actions like the Jewish Passover (verses 26–29). This institution narrative can easily be detached from the unit which surrounds it, since it was probably part of a larger eucharistic prayer celebrated in the church to which Matthew wrote. Like the Passover meal, each time this Last Supper is celebrated, the founding event is renewed and made present again. In these words and gestures, Jesus expresses the meaning of his own death. The "blood of the covenant" is drawn from Exodus 24, which narrates God's ratification of the covenant with Israel. This blood of Jesus, which will be poured out in his death on the cross, becomes the blood bond between God and his people. His words over the cup affirm that his death is the ultimate redeeming act, "for the forgiveness of sins," liberating humanity from its most powerful bondage.

The Last Supper, like all previous Passover meals, not only remembers the past but also anticipates the future. Jesus looks forward to the day when he will drink from the cup with his disciples in the Father's kingdom (verse 29). References to the Passover, the covenant, the forgiveness of sins, and the kingdom of God all focus the attention of Matthew's listeners on the profound significance of this commemorative ritual of Jesus which initiates the passion account. The hymn that concludes the Passover meal, the Hallel (Pss 114–118), gives thanks to God for constant faithfulness in redeeming his people. With thanksgiving on their lips, the disciples proceed with Jesus to the Mount of Olives.

Though the Last Supper affirms Jesus' bond with his disciples, that bond is severely tested afterward. The mood of the scene turns somber when Jesus tells his disciples that they will all desert him and scatter that very night (verse 31). Yet, their abandonment of Jesus will not be final, since he promises to gather them and lead them like a shepherd in Galilee after his resurrection (verse 32). Peter, the first disciple called, insists with great bravado that he would be the last person to desert Jesus. When Jesus tells Peter that he will not only desert Jesus but will deny him three times, Peter adamantly adds that he would die before denying Jesus. The mention of the strutting, crowing rooster creates an image that expresses Peter's impetuous and boastful claims.

Though all the disciples reject the possibility of deserting and denying Jesus, the scene in Gethsemane shows how the disciples fall asleep rather than pray with Jesus and flee at the moment of his arrest. In contrast to his disciples, Jesus shows himself to be faithful and obedient to the Father's will. Jesus prays in words reminiscent of Psalm 42, a psalm of lament which expresses a longing for God in the midst of great sorrow and distress. Jesus prays to "my Father," expressing the extraordinary intimacy he enjoyed with God (verses 39, 42). The prayer is both a prayer for deliverance from death, "let this cup pass from me," and a resolute commitment to God's will, "not what I want but what you want." His prostrate position on the ground emphasizes his intense supplication and his submission to the Father.

This threefold prayer of Jesus is met with his threefold return to find his disciples sleeping. Their three lost opportunities to stay alert anticipate Peter's three lost opportunities to confess his discipleship. In his passion, Jesus shows himself to be the model of prayer and faithfulness for the later church. His watchful obedience contrasts with the drowsy unpreparedness of the disciples. Jesus triumphs in the face of trial, and the disciples enter into temptation and flee.

## Reflection and Discussion

• When the community of disciples celebrates Jesus' Passover meal in the Eucharist, what elements remember the past? What elements anticipate the future?

• Why is the rooster such an apt image for Peter?

• What does the example of Jesus in Gethsemane teach me about prayer? When has it been most difficult for me to pray, "Your will be done"?

## Prayer

*Jesus, your prayer at Gethsemane shows your intimacy with the Father and your submission to his will. Help me stay alert and awake as I live as your disciple, and teach me how to pray for a knowledge and acceptance of the Father's will for me.*

"Do you think that I cannot appeal to my Father, and he will at once send me more than twelve legions of angels? But how then would the scriptures be fulfilled, which say it must happen in this way?"

Matt 26:53–54

# The Arrest and Interrogation of Jesus

**MATTHEW 26:47–75** *⁴⁷While he was still speaking, Judas, one of the twelve, arrived; with him was a large crowd with swords and clubs, from the chief priests and the elders of the people. ⁴⁸Now the betrayer had given them a sign, saying, "The one I will kiss is the man; arrest him." ⁴⁹At once he came up to Jesus and said, "Greetings, Rabbi!" and kissed him. ⁵⁰Jesus said to him, "Friend, do what you are here to do." Then they came and laid hands on Jesus and arrested him. ⁵¹Suddenly, one of those with Jesus put his hand on his sword, drew it, and struck the slave of the high priest, cutting off his ear. ⁵²Then Jesus said to him, "Put your sword back into its place; for all who take the sword will perish by the sword. ⁵³Do you think that I cannot appeal to my Father, and he will at once send me more than twelve legions of angels? ⁵⁴But how then would the scriptures be fulfilled, which say it must happen in this way?" ⁵⁵At that hour Jesus said to the crowds, "Have you come out with swords and clubs to arrest me as though I were a bandit? Day after day I sat in the temple teaching, and you did not arrest me. ⁵⁶But all this has taken place, so that the scriptures of the prophets may be fulfilled." Then all the disciples deserted him and fled.*

⁵⁷*Those who had arrested Jesus took him to Caiaphas the high priest, in whose house the scribes and the elders had gathered.* ⁵⁸*But Peter was following him at a distance, as far as the courtyard of the high priest; and going inside, he sat with the guards in order to see how this would end.* ⁵⁹*Now the chief priests and the whole council were looking for false testimony against Jesus so that they might put him to death,* ⁶⁰*but they found none, though many false witnesses came forward. At last two came forward* ⁶¹*and said, "This fellow said, 'I am able to destroy the temple of God and to build it in three days.'"* ⁶²*The high priest stood up and said, "Have you no answer? What is it that they testify against you?"* ⁶³*But Jesus was silent. Then the high priest said to him, "I put you under oath before the living God, tell us if you are the Messiah, the Son of God."* ⁶⁴*Jesus said to him, "You have said so. But I tell you,*

> *From now on you will see the Son of Man*
> *seated at the right hand of Power*
> *and coming on the clouds of heaven."*

⁶⁵*Then the high priest tore his clothes and said, "He has blasphemed! Why do we still need witnesses? You have now heard his blasphemy.* ⁶⁶*What is your verdict?" They answered, "He deserves death."* ⁶⁷*Then they spat in his face and struck him; and some slapped him,* ⁶⁸*saying, "Prophesy to us, you Messiah! Who is it that struck you?"*

⁶⁹*Now Peter was sitting outside in the courtyard. A servant-girl came to him and said, "You also were with Jesus the Galilean."* ⁷⁰*But he denied it before all of them, saying, "I do not know what you are talking about."* ⁷¹*When he went out to the porch, another servant-girl saw him, and she said to the bystanders, "This man was with Jesus of Nazareth."* ⁷²*Again he denied it with an oath, "I do not know the man."* ⁷³*After a little while the bystanders came up and said to Peter, "Certainly you are also one of them, for your accent betrays you."* ⁷⁴*Then he began to curse, and he swore an oath, "I do not know the man!" At that moment the cock crowed.* ⁷⁵*Then Peter remembered what Jesus had said: "Before the cock crows, you will deny me three times." And he went out and wept bitterly.*

Following Judas' kiss of betrayal, Jesus addresses him as "friend" and says, "Do what you are here to do" (verse 50). Jesus shows his command of the situation and his awareness of his fate. In effect, Jesus is giving permission for the final events to begin. As Jesus is seized and arrested,

one of the disciples lashes out at the crowd with his sword. This violent reac-
tion gives Jesus the opportunity to reaffirm the non-violent stance he taught
in the sermon on the mount. He rejects the retaliatory response, and proclaims, "All who take the sword will perish by the sword" (verse 52). If Jesus
wishes, he could resist with the forces of heaven, with twelve legions of angels.
But Jesus has committed himself to carry out his Father's will, the costly path
which began to be unfolded in the prophets of Scripture (verses 54, 56).
Following this path throughout his life, Jesus had often withdrawn in the face
of hostility and gone another way. But now, as his passion begins, Jesus neither
withdraws nor confronts, but freely surrenders to violent aggression in order
to overcome it in the way laid down by God. In the face of such resolute submission, "all the disciples deserted him and fled," just as Jesus said they
would.

The narrative of Jesus' questioning by the high priest and his council
exposes the sordid nature of the proceeding. Their intention was to obtain
false testimony against Jesus so that he could be put to death (verse 59).
Finally two men came forward to testify that Jesus claimed to be able to
destroy the temple and rebuild it in three days (verse 61). The claim is false in
that, although Jesus performed a prophetic act of judgment on the temple and
remarked about its coming destruction, he did not say that he himself could
or would destroy it. Yet the statement is also ironically true in that the destruction and restoration of the temple were thought to be a sign of the messianic
age. If fact, Jesus had stated that his presence is "greater than the temple"
(12:6) and his teachings associate his own death with the destruction of the
temple. When the high priest demands that Jesus state under oath whether he
is "the Messiah, the Son of God," Jesus responds affirmatively. In addition he
adds that he is "the Son of Man seated at the right hand of Power," an
announcement of his divine authority and his future coming in triumphant
glory (verse 64). Jesus' "treasonous" claims about the temple and his "blasphemous" claim to be the Messiah, Son of God, and triumphant Son of Man are
the direct causes of his condemnation to death by the religious leaders.

As Jesus is arrested and brought to the house of the high priest, Peter follows at a distance into the courtyard. The narrative of Peter surrounds the
scene of Jesus' interrogation before the high priest's council. In this way the
gospel suggests that the two scenes are occurring simultaneously. As Jesus is
confronted by verbal threats from the high priest and remains steadfast, Peter

is tested by servants and cowers in fear and denial. He is accused of being "with Jesus" (verse 69, 71). The same phrase is used in other scenes to indicate the intimate bond that existed between Jesus and his disciples. It is his belonging to Jesus, a relationship built up and enriched through many experiences, which Peter denies in his weakness.

The drama builds in intensity as the threefold denial gradually escalates to a powerful climax. First, Peter denies "before all of them" that he even knows what the servant-girl is talking about (verse 70). Then, questioned by another servant-girl, he explicitly declares with an oath that he does not know Jesus (verse 72). Finally when the bystanders come over to accuse him, Peter begins to curse and he swears with an oath, "I do not know the man!" (verse 74). As the drama is mounting, Peter is gradually retreating: at first he is "sitting outside in the courtyard," then he moves "out to the porch," and finally he flees the scene after realizing the horror of what he has done. The rooster's crow, piercing the darkness of those early hours, forces Peter to recognize the tragedy of his denial.

## Reflection and Discussion

• What does it tell me about Jesus that he is able to call upon legions of angels? What does it tell me about Jesus that he chooses not to do so?

• What do other New Testament writings add to the understanding of Matthew's text about the destruction and restoration of the temple by Jesus (see John 2:21; Eph 2:19–22; 1 Pet 2:4–8)?

• How does Matthew contrast the interrogation of Jesus with the interrogation of Peter? What is the effect on his readers?

• What is the effect of the crowing rooster on Peter? Why will Peter always remember the cock's crow?

• The story of Peter's denials has helped struggling Christians through the ages. What do Peter's denials teach me?

## Prayer

*Messiah and Son of God, you could have called on legions of angels to help you in your agony, but you chose to submit to your antagonists and suffer in commitment to God's plan foretold in Scripture. Teach me to trust in the Father's will for my life.*

# SUGGESTIONS FOR FACILITATORS, GROUP SESSION 5

1. Welcome group members and ask if anyone has any questions, announcements, or requests.

2. You may want to pray this prayer as a group:

*Father of our Lord Jesus, you gave us your Son to fulfill your word in the Scriptures and to fulfill your plan for the world. He is the Bridegroom for whom we keep our lamps burning, the Master who disperses talents to be used for the kingdom, the King who is present in the least ones, the Son of Man who will come in glory, and the Son of God who suffers to redeem us from sin. Help us to stay alert and watchful as we live our lives as disciples of Jesus, and keep us prayerful as we seek to live according to your will.*

3. Ask one or more of the following questions:
   - What most intrigued you from this week's study?
   - What makes you want to know and understand more of God's word?

4. Discuss lessons 19 through 24. Choose one or more of the questions for reflection and discussion from each lesson to talk over as a group.

5. Ask the group members to name one thing they have most appreciated about the way the group has worked during this Bible study. Ask group members to discuss any changes they might suggest in the way the group works in future studies.

6. Invite group members to complete lessons 25 through 30 on their own during the six days before the next meeting. They should write out their own answers to the questions as preparation for next week's session.

7. Ask group members how the study of the gospel effects their hearing and response to the gospel proclaimed in liturgy.

8. Conclude by praying aloud together the prayer at the end of one of the lessons discussed. You may want to conclude the prayer by asking members to voice prayers of thanksgiving.

Now Jesus stood before the governor; and the governor asked him,
"Are you the King of the Jews?" Matt 27:11

# The Fate of Judas

MATTHEW 27:1–14 ¹*When morning came, all the chief priests and the elders of the people conferred together against Jesus in order to bring about his death. ²They bound him, led him away, and handed him over to Pilate the governor.*

*³When Judas, his betrayer, saw that Jesus was condemned, he repented and brought back the thirty pieces of silver to the chief priests and the elders. ⁴He said, "I have sinned by betraying innocent blood." But they said, "What is that to us? See to it yourself." ⁵Throwing down the pieces of silver in the temple, he departed; and he went and hanged himself. ⁶But the chief priests, taking the pieces of silver, said, "It is not lawful to put them into the treasury, since they are blood money." ⁷After conferring together, they used them to buy the potter's field as a place to bury foreigners. ⁸For this reason that field has been called the Field of Blood to this day. ⁹Then was fulfilled what had been spoken through the prophet Jeremiah, "And they took the thirty pieces of silver, the price of the one on whom a price had been set, on whom some of the people of Israel had set a price, ¹⁰and they gave them for the potter's field, as the Lord commanded me."*

*¹¹Now Jesus stood before the governor; and the governor asked him, "Are you the King of the Jews?" Jesus said, "You say so." ¹²But when he was accused by the chief priests and elders, he did not answer. ¹³Then Pilate said to him, "Do you not hear how many accusations they make against you?" ¹⁴But he gave him no answer, not even to a single charge, so that the governor was greatly amazed.*

After a long night of questioning and mockery, the council of religious leaders has reached its official decision that Jesus should be put to death. They restrain him and transfer him to the jurisdiction of Pilate, the Roman prefect. Though he lives in Caesarea on the coast, Pilate stays in Jerusalem during Passover and other feasts when the city is filled with crowds and religious fervor. He is responsible for keeping the peace and preventing any riots or revolts against Roman rule. As the representative of the government of Rome, he holds the political and military power, and holds the authority to order executions.

Seeing Jesus condemned to death, Judas deeply regrets his betrayal. He recognizes his mistake in betraying innocent blood and returns the thirty pieces of silver (verse 3). Matthew deliberately avoids using the standard word for repentance, in order to show that Judas' regret was probably not a deep conversion of heart. The temple authorities rebuff Judas, saying that his sin is his own problem, and Judas gives in to despair. Characteristically Matthew sees the betrayal of Judas, the return of the silver pieces to the temple, and the purchase of the burial field as enveloped by scriptural fulfillment. The ancient prophets spoke of a pattern of rejection that finds its ultimate fulfillment in the rejection of Jesus.

By recounting the last action of both Peter and Judas in the passion narrative, Matthew sets up a strong contrast. Peter "went out and wept bitterly," while Judas "went and hanged himself" (verse 5). While Peter's act is despicable, he will return to the following of Jesus and resume the role assigned to him. But Judas, though he acknowledges his sin, never seeks the forgiveness of Jesus or rejoins the disciples. Peter recovers and serves the church as its "rock," while Judas hangs himself and hopelessly swings in the wind. The failures of these two prominent disciples and their different ultimate fates provide both a warning and a message of hope for the future church.

The central question of the trial before Pilate concerns the kingship of Jesus: "Are you the King of the Jews?" (verse 11). Pilate's loyalty to the Roman emperor requires him to investigate any potential rivals to royal power. The claim to kingship is treason against the empire, a crime punishable by death. The title "king of the Jews" is used only by Gentiles in Matthew's gospel. It will be used again by the soldiers to mock Jesus and it will be the inscription placed on the cross. Jesus' response to Pilate, "You say so," is both an affirmation that Jesus is truly the king and a disassociation from the political sense intended by Pilate. In the face of the ongoing questioning, Jesus remains silent. What is a judge to do with an accused criminal who has not pleaded guilty but who does not assert innocence or deny the charges against him when he is questioned (verse 14)? Pilate is stunned.

## Reflection and Discussion

• What seems to be the primary difference in the response of Peter and Judas to their shameful acts?

• What causes one person to despair and another to repent? What does the contrast between Judas and Peter teach me about responding to failure?

• In what sense is Jesus a king and in what sense is he not a king?

## Prayer

*Lord Jesus, I have often been unfaithful to you and denied my discipleship. May I always return to you after my failures and receive your merciful forgiveness. I ask you to reign over my life.*

They stripped him and put a scarlet robe on him, and
after twisting some thorns into a crown, they put it on his head.

Matt 27:28–29

# The Trial of Jesus Before Pilate

**MATTHEW 27:15–31** *15Now at the festival the governor was accustomed to release a prisoner for the crowd, anyone whom they wanted. 16At that time they had a notorious prisoner, called Jesus Barabbas. 17So after they had gathered, Pilate said to them, "Whom do you want me to release for you, Jesus Barabbas or Jesus who is called the Messiah?" 18For he realized that it was out of jealousy that they had handed him over. 19While he was sitting on the judgment seat, his wife sent word to him, "Have nothing to do with that innocent man, for today I have suffered a great deal because of a dream about him." 20Now the chief priests and the elders persuaded the crowds to ask for Barabbas and to have Jesus killed. 21The governor again said to them, "Which of the two do you want me to release for you?" And they said, "Barabbas." 22Pilate said to them, "Then what should I do with Jesus who is called the Messiah?" All of them said, "Let him be crucified!" 23Then he asked, "Why, what evil has he done?" But they shouted all the more, "Let him be crucified!"*

*24So when Pilate saw that he could do nothing, but rather that a riot was beginning, he took some water and washed his hands before the crowd, saying, "I am innocent of this man's blood; see to it yourselves." 25Then the people*

*as a whole answered, "His blood be on us and on our children!"* [26]*So he released Barabbas for them; and after flogging Jesus, he handed him over to be
crucified.*

[27]*Then the soldiers of the governor took Jesus into the governor's headquar-
ters, and they gathered the whole cohort around him.* [28]*They stripped him and
put a scarlet robe on him,* [29]*and after twisting some thorns into a crown, they
put it on his head. They put a reed in his right hand and knelt before him and
mocked him, saying, "Hail, King of the Jews!"* [30]*They spat on him, and took the
reed and struck him on the head.* [31]*After mocking him, they stripped him of the
robe and put his own clothes on him. Then they led him away to crucify him.*

The custom of releasing a prisoner at Passover was a concession to the
Jews, a conciliatory gesture on the part of the Roman government.
Nationalistic fervor ran high during the feast of Israel's liberation, and
allowing the Jews to choose a prisoner for release was meant to cool their pas-
sions. The gospel builds up this scene as the climactic choice of the passion
account. The choice of clear: Jesus Barabbas or Jesus the Messiah (verses 17,
21). The historical choice in Jerusalem represents the continual choice that
everyone must make. When confronted with Jesus and his message, people
must ultimately choose to accept or reject him.

Pilate is a cowardly official who abdicates his responsibility, a vacillating
judge who allows himself to be swayed by others. He realizes that the charges
against Jesus are bogus and that Jesus has been handed over to him by the
religious leaders "out of jealousy" (verse 18). The leaders have persuaded the
crowds to choose Barabbas for release and to call for Jesus' death, and Pilate
accedes to their demands only after repeated, failed attempts to dissuade the
crowds. Pilate's dilemma is intensified by the communication of his wife's
dream, which convinced her of Jesus' innocence (verse 19). In Matthew's gospel, dreams are a vehicle of divine revelations, as seen in the dreams of Joseph
and of the Magi in the infancy narratives. Perhaps Pilate's wife represents the
divine voice people can hear in those they love, urging them to do the right
and to act with integrity. Despite his wife's warning, Pilate gives in to the
crowds when he realizes he is unable to convince them of Jesus' innocence
and that a riot is breaking out. As the shouts of the crowd grow louder, Pilate
gives in because it is expedient to do so. His symbolic hand-washing is a

pathetic, hypocritical gesture (verse 24). Pilate is the only figure who can authorize a crucifixion, and he must share the guilt for Jesus' death.

The religious leaders and the people of Jerusalem must also take responsibility for the death of Jesus. Their declaration, "His blood be on us and on our children!" is an expression of responsibility for the shedding of blood. A text from Jeremiah is particularly important for understanding this declaration of the people. The prophet warns "all the officials and all the people" not to kill him, stating, "You will be bringing innocent blood upon yourselves and upon this city and its inhabitants" (Jer 26:12, 15). For Matthew's gospel, the rejection and death of Jesus is one more instance in the history of Israel's rejection of prophetic messengers sent by God. The distorted view that this declaration of responsibility constitutes a blood libel for all Jews of all times is clearly false.

So Jesus is again "handed over": Judas had handed him over to the chief priests, the priests had handed him over to Pilate, and Pilate "handed him over to be crucified" (verse 26). The disciples, the Jewish leaders, and the Roman authorities all share in the responsibility for Jesus' death. Even the crowds share responsibility. There are no mere spectators.

The Roman soldiers who mock and torture Jesus were trained to subdue and oppress people in the far corners of the empire and were conscripted for crucifixion duty. The scarlet cloak and the twisted crown of thorns, along with the reed placed in his right hand to imitate a royal scepter, ridicule the claim to royal status made about him. The mock coronation and mock homage acclaim Jesus with the same title used in the accusations against him during his trial: "Hail, King of the Jews" (verse 29). The soldiers' sarcastic shout is a cruel parody of the "Hail Caesar" acclamation offered to the Roman emperor.

Given the repeated affirmations of Jesus as the royal Messiah throughout the gospel, the irony of this scene is acute. Of course, Jesus truly is the king of both the Jews and the Gentiles, and his mockery proclaims the truth of his identity. He is the King of the people of Jerusalem and of the whole Roman Empire, and at his name every knee will bow. The brutality of the scene typifies the violence of the empire and is in direct contrast to the nonviolent teachings of Jesus. As his tormentors kneel before him and hail him as king, the readers of the gospel know that he is a king in a manner totally different from expectations. He is the king who is "humble and mounted on a donkey" (21:5), the king who "will sit on the throne of his glory" and "all the nations will be gathered before him" (25:31–32).

## Reflection and Discussion

• What is Pilate's overriding concern in this trial? What do I do to appease the crowds?

• Jesus accepted the penalty for the crimes of Barabbas. In what way does Barabbas represent me in the passion account?

• Why is it impossible to blame the death of Jesus on any one group of people?

## Prayer

*Suffering King, you were mocked, tormented, and handed over to crucifixion in order to satisfy the crowds. Help me to hand over my whole self to you, not to satisfy others but to give glory to you. Reign over my life from your glorious cross.*

Over his head they put the charge against him, which read,
"This is Jesus, the King of the Jews." Matt 27:37

# The Crucifixion, Mockery, and Death of Jesus

**MATTHEW 27:32–56** *32As they went out, they came upon a man from Cyrene named Simon; they compelled this man to carry his cross. 33And when they came to a place called Golgotha (which means Place of a Skull), 34they offered him wine to drink, mixed with gall; but when he tasted it, he would not drink it. 35And when they had crucified him, they divided his clothes among themselves by casting lots; 36then they sat down there and kept watch over him. 37Over his head they put the charge against him, which read, "This is Jesus, the King of the Jews."*

*38Then two bandits were crucified with him, one on his right and one on his left. 39Those who passed by derided him, shaking their heads 40and saying, "You who would destroy the temple and build it in three days, save yourself! If you are the Son of God, come down from the cross." 41In the same way the chief priests also, along with the scribes and elders, were mocking him, saying, 42"He saved others; he cannot save himself. He is the King of Israel; let him come down from the cross now, and we will believe in him. 43He trusts in God; let God deliver him now, if he wants to; for he said, 'I am God's Son.'" 44The bandits who were crucified with him also taunted him in the same way.*

*45From noon on, darkness came over the whole land until three in the afternoon. 46And about three o'clock Jesus cried with a loud voice, "Eli, Eli, lema*

109

*sabachthani?" that is, "My God, my God, why have you forsaken me?"* [47] *When some of the bystanders heard it, they said, "This man is calling for Elijah."* [48] *At once one of them ran and got a sponge, filled it with sour wine, put it on a stick, and gave it to him to drink.* [49] *But the others said, "Wait, let us see whether Elijah will come to save him."* [50] *Then Jesus cried again with a loud voice and breathed his last.* [51] *At that moment the curtain of the temple was torn in two, from top to bottom. The earth shook, and the rocks were split.* [52] *The tombs also were opened, and many bodies of the saints who had fallen asleep were raised.* [53] *After his resurrection they came out of the tombs and entered the holy city and appeared to many.* [54] *Now when the centurion and those with him, who were keeping watch over Jesus, saw the earthquake and what took place, they were terrified and said, "Truly this man was God's Son!"*

[55] *Many women were also there, looking on from a distance; they had followed Jesus from Galilee and had provided for him.* [56] *Among them were Mary Magdalene, and Mary the mother of James and Joseph, and the mother of the sons of Zebedee.*

The passion account reaches its climax with the crucifixion and death of Jesus. Because execution could not be carried out within the walls of the holy city, Jesus was taken outside Jerusalem to a site called Golgotha, a skull-shaped rock formation that gave rise to its name. The gospel does not dwell on the physical suffering of Jesus. The horrors of crucifixion were well known to the community to whom Matthew wrote. Instead, he focuses on the meaning of Jesus' suffering and death and how the whole event fulfilled the ancient Scriptures.

After Jesus is crucified, a placard is placed over his head which reads, "This is Jesus, the King of the Jews" (verse 37). The name of "Jesus" affixed to the cross is significant, especially since Matthew had interpreted his name early in the gospel: "You are to name him Jesus, for he will save his people from their sins" (1:21). And again, the title "King of the Jews" becomes an ironic proclamation of the truth of his sovereignty. The two bandits crucified with him, one on his right and one on his left, become his royal court. The crucifixion of Jesus is the fullest expression of his royal power to save his people from their sins.

The scene is thick with sarcastic mockery. Jesus is derided first by the passers-by who mock his claims over the temple. Next, the religious leaders ridicule him as "King of Israel." Finally, the two crucified on either side of Jesus revile him in the same way. As Jesus was tempted three times by the devil at the beginning of his public ministry (4:1–11), he is mocked three times at his death. Both the devil and the mockers focus on his identity and mission as God's Son, tempting him with the alternative of ruling without suffering. At the cross, Jesus experiences once again the demonic presence, which tells him to "come down from the cross" (verses 40, 42). The mockery is again palpably ironic since Jesus is truly the messianic King, the Son of God. The temple will indeed be destroyed and restored in the resurrection, Jesus is the King of Israel who saves his people, he is the Son who trusts in God. He does not come down from the cross, but pours out his blood in the new covenant and will overcome death in his resurrection. Since the gospel shows every detail of the derision to be true, the mockers are unsuspecting evangelizers, proclaiming the deepest truths of Jesus' identity and mission.

The cry of Jesus from the cross is the first line of Psalm 22, quoted first in Hebrew (verse 46). Though the bystanders think Jesus is calling on Elijah, since the name of the prophet is derived from the same Hebrew word as "Eli," Jesus is actually praying a desperate prayer that he knows well from Scripture. The words come instinctively to Jesus' mind to express his experience of torment and his feeling of abandonment. His suffering is not just physical torture, but emotional and spiritual anguish as well. Yet, by quoting the first verse of the psalm, the evangelist wants the reader to recall the entire psalm and know that Jesus continued the psalm as his final prayer to the Father. Several other verses of the psalm are quoted or alluded to in the passion account, showing that Jesus is the fullest embodiment of the faithful Israelite. Like the psalmist, Jesus is scorned and abandoned by his friends and seemingly by God, he is mocked and tormented by enemies, his clothing is divided by lot, his hands and feet are pierced, he thirsts for a drink, and he places his life solely in God's hands. Then after expressing the desolation of his suffering, the second half of the psalm focuses on the triumphant vindication of God's faithful one who is delivered from death, gives praise to God who hears his cry, and receives the praise of nations and future generations. In this way, the gospel demonstrates that the cross of Jesus is no unfortunate coincidence of circumstances, but the working out of God's saving purposes for which people have waited and longed for generations.

Matthew's gospel makes it clear that the death of Jesus and his anticipated resurrection constitute the climactic act of salvation history. The shaking earth and splitting rocks, the opening of tombs, the resurrection and appearance of the saints, these are all events prophesied for the end of the age and the breaking in of God's kingdom. The saints who are raised represent the holy ones of the Old Testament. Though the death and resurrection of Jesus brings forth a new people, God does not forsake the saints of Israel. The climactic confession of faith in Jesus, "Truly this man was God's Son," is made by all who are keeping watch over Jesus (verse 54). The community of faith formed at the cross, Gentile soldiers and Jewish women, represents the beginning of the new community for a new era.

## Reflection and Discussion

• In what ways does the mockery of Jesus on the cross echo the temptations of Jesus in the desert? In what ways do the devil and the mockers proclaim who Jesus truly is?

• What is my understanding of Jesus' loud cry from the cross? What does it teach me about the sorrow and hope of Jesus' final moments before his death?

## Prayer

*Son of God, you did not come down from the cross, but you suffered and died to save the world from sin. Let me never be ashamed of you who accepted so much shame and suffering for me.*

**Joseph took the body and wrapped it in a clean linen cloth and laid it in his own new tomb, which he had hewn in the rock.**

Matt 27:59–60

# Vigil at the Tomb of Jesus

**MATTHEW 27:57–66** *⁵⁷When it was evening, there came a rich man from Arimathea, named Joseph, who was also a disciple of Jesus. ⁵⁸He went to Pilate and asked for the body of Jesus; then Pilate ordered it to be given to him. ⁵⁹So Joseph took the body and wrapped it in a clean linen cloth ⁶⁰and laid it in his own new tomb, which he had hewn in the rock. He then rolled a great stone to the door of the tomb and went away. ⁶¹Mary Magdalene and the other Mary were there, sitting opposite the tomb.*

*⁶²The next day, that is, after the day of Preparation, the chief priests and the Pharisees gathered before Pilate ⁶³and said, "Sir, we remember what that impostor said while he was still alive, 'After three days I will rise again.' ⁶⁴Therefore command the tomb to be made secure until the third day; otherwise his disciples may go and steal him away, and tell the people, 'He has been raised from the dead,' and the last deception would be worse than the first." ⁶⁵Pilate said to them, "You have a guard of soldiers; go, make it as secure as you can." ⁶⁶So they went with the guard and made the tomb secure by sealing the stone.*

These two scenes, the burial of Jesus and the securing of the tomb, serve as a transition between the death of Jesus on the cross and his resurrection. The Romans often left the bodies at the site of crucifixion for the birds and wild beasts to scavenge. But according to Jewish practice, a body should not be left on the cross overnight (Deut 21:22–23), and the law forbade burial after the Sabbath had begun. Since Jesus died on a Friday, at about three o'clock in the afternoon, and the Sabbath began at sundown, there was little time.

The narrative begins by introducing another disciple of Jesus, a rich man named Joseph from Arimathea. Unlike the rich young man from earlier in the gospel, Joseph became a disciple and now uses his wealth to help the poor and serve the needs of others. This he does for Jesus by using his influence to go to Pilate requesting the body and by burying Jesus in his own rock-hewn tomb. Joseph gives Jesus a proper burial, doing what the other male disciples of Jesus should have been there to do. He wraps the body in clean linen, places it in his new tomb, and rolls a great stone across the tomb's entrance (verse 60).

The women disciples, who had been following Jesus from Galilee, serve as faithful witnesses from the conclusion of the crucifixion account, through the burial scene where they are sitting opposite the sepulcher witnessing the entombment, and on to their discovery of the empty tomb and the first encounter with Christ in his resurrection. These women are identified at the tomb as "Mary Magdalene and the other Mary," earlier identified at the cross as the mother of James and Joseph. These women are still keeping watch over the body as Joseph departs. They are the last to leave the tomb and they will be the first to discover it empty.

The next day, on the Sabbath, the religious leaders go to Pilate with a request they do not want to delay. Somehow they had become aware of Jesus' promise to rise from the dead after three days (verse 63). They call Jesus an "impostor" and fear that his disciples will steal his body and perpetrate a resurrection hoax. The leaders request that Pilate have the tomb sealed and guarded. Pilate places his soldiers at their disposal and tells the leaders, "Make it as secure as you can" (verse 65). Fixing a seal to the stone involved pouring clay or molten wax between the stone and the tomb and then imprinting the still-soft wax or clay with a signet ring. Anyone entering the tomb would crack the seal, but an unbroken seal would indicate that no one had moved the stone. Ironically, the more efforts the leaders make to prevent tampering with Jesus' body, the more implausible becomes their deceptive claim that his disciples stole it. The scene prepares for the resurrection narrative since no matter how securely the tomb is guarded, the victorious and resurrected Jesus cannot be contained in the grave.

## Reflection and Discussion

• How does Joseph of Arimathea demonstrate that a rich person can be a disciple of Jesus? What do I, as a disciple, do with my riches?

• What might have gone through the minds of the two Marys as they sat facing the tomb of Jesus?

• How do people sometimes place a guard over their mind and heart in order to prevent the risen Jesus from breaking through into their lives?

## Prayer

*Lord Jesus, your rock-hewn tomb could not contain the life within it. Though I often close my life from you and hide from your presence, give me the grace to open my mind and heart to the power of your risen life.*

Suddenly there was a great earthquake;
for an angel of the Lord, descending from heaven,
came and rolled back the stone and sat on it.
Matt 28:2

# Discovery of the Empty Tomb and Appearance of Jesus

**MATTHEW 28:1–10** *¹After the sabbath, as the first day of the week was dawning, Mary Magdalene and the other Mary went to see the tomb. ²And suddenly there was a great earthquake; for an angel of the Lord, descending from heaven, came and rolled back the stone and sat on it. ³His appearance was like lightning, and his clothing white as snow. ⁴For fear of him the guards shook and became like dead men. ⁵But the angel said to the women, "Do not be afraid; I know that you are looking for Jesus who was crucified. ⁶He is not here; for he has been raised, as he said. Come, see the place where he lay. ⁷Then go quickly and tell his disciples, 'He has been raised from the dead, and indeed he is going ahead of you to Galilee; there you will see him.' This is my message for you." ⁸So they left the tomb quickly with fear and great joy, and ran to tell his disciples. ⁹Suddenly Jesus met them and said, "Greetings!" And they came to him, took hold of his feet, and worshiped him. ¹⁰Then Jesus said to them, "Do not be afraid; go and tell my brothers to go to Galilee; there they will see me."*

When the two Marys return to the tomb as daylight dawns on Sunday, there is a great earthquake as an angel descends and rolls back the stone from the tomb. The earthquake points to the world-changing and earth-shattering implications of the resurrection of Israel's Messiah. The signs that interpreted the death of Jesus on the cross continue, tying together the death and resurrection into one great final event marking the new and decisive age of salvation. The seismic repercussions of that earthquake continue to reverberate down through the course of history. Though its magnitude rocks the very foundations of the earth, its impact is not destructive, but life-creating and hope-inducing.

In Jewish and early Christian writings, an angel is a messenger of God's word and an agent of God's deeds. The action of the glorious angel in rolling back the stone and sitting upon it triumphantly expresses the fact that the resurrection is the achievement of God, his triumph over death in the resurrection of his Son (verse 2). There is no indication that the angel rolled back the stone to let Jesus out of the tomb. Surely there is no barrier to the Risen Lord. But the stone was rolled away for the sake of the women, so they could see that the tomb was empty.

Matthew's gospel begins and ends with angels; they announce both the birth and the resurrection of Jesus. In contrast to the deadening fear of the guards, the angel tells the women, "Do not be afraid." The angel then proclaims the core of the gospel: Jesus who was crucified is no longer in the place of death. "He has been raised." Then the angel gives the women a mission: "Go quickly." They are to proclaim the message of the resurrection to the disciples and tell them that Jesus is going before them to Galilee where they will see him.

As the women are running to announce the good news to the disciples, Jesus meets them on the way. They grasp his feet and worship him, demonstrating that the risen presence of Jesus is a real, yet transformed person, and not just a disembodied spirit or vivid memory. Jesus does not allow them to linger in adoration, but encourages them on their mission as the first witnesses and evangelizers of the resurrection. The commission of Jesus to the women is basically the same as that given to them by the angel, except Jesus calls the disciples "my brothers." This indicates his forgiveness of the disciples for their failure and his restoration of them to full fellowship with himself. The women fulfill their mission and their authority as bearers of the message of resurrection is unchallenged.

## Reflection and Discussion

• Why would the angel first announce the resurrection to the women and why would Jesus appear first to the women rather than to the male disciples?

• The women experienced "fear and great joy" when given their mission by the angel. Is it possible to experience these two emotions simultaneously? When have I felt both great joy and deep fear?

• How would I argue against the idea, which some believe, that the disciples stole the body of Jesus and devised a resurrection hoax?

## Prayer

*Risen Lord, I fear the awesome power manifested at your resurrection and I rejoice in the good news of your rising. I want to grasp your feet and worship you, but you have sent me to bring the good news to your people. Please urge me on the way.*

"Go therefore and make disciples of all nations,
baptizing them in the name of the Father and of the Son
and of the Holy Spirit, and teaching them to obey everything
that I have commanded you." Matt 28:19–20

# Commission to All the Nations by the Risen Lord

**MATTHEW 28:11–20** [11]*While they were going, some of the guard went into the city and told the chief priests everything that had happened.* [12]*After the priests had assembled with the elders, they devised a plan to give a large sum of money to the soldiers,* [13]*telling them, "You must say, 'His disciples came by night and stole him away while we were asleep.'* [14]*If this comes to the governor's ears, we will satisfy him and keep you out of trouble."* [15]*So they took the money and did as they were directed. And this story is still told among the Jews to this day.*

[16]*Now the eleven disciples went to Galilee, to the mountain to which Jesus had directed them.* [17]*When they saw him, they worshiped him; but some doubted.* [18]*And Jesus came and said to them, "All authority in heaven and on earth has been given to me.* [19]*Go therefore and make disciples of all nations, baptizing them in the name of the Father and of the Son and of the Holy Spirit,* [20]*and teaching them to obey everything that I have commanded you. And remember, I am with you always, to the end of the age."*

A	s the women go to tell the good news of the resurrection to the other disciples, the Roman guards are going to report the resurrection to the chief priests. The guards and the official seal on the tomb could not prevent the removal of Jesus' body because it was not stolen by the disciples but raised by the Father. By telling "everything that had happened," they too become unwitting evangelizers of the Christian message. The religious leaders, having feared that the disciples would concoct a resurrection hoax, now must fabricate a story themselves. To make sure everyone sticks to the story, the soldiers are persuaded with "a large sum of money" (verse 12). As they had bribed Judas at the beginning of the passion account, now they bribe the guards to lie about the resurrection.

The leaders in Jerusalem want Jesus to remain dead in the eyes of the people. The guards are paid to lie and say they were asleep when the disciples came and stole the body of Jesus at night (verse 13). The religious leaders promise to protect them in case a report of their negligence should reach the ears of Pilate. After bribing Judas, they now bribe the guards, and they may need to bribe Pilate too. As the guards took the money, the story that the disciples stole the body of Jesus began to spread, a falsehood that was still being told decades later when Matthew wrote his gospel (verse 15).

The grand finale of Matthew's gospel occurs back in Galilee, where Jesus first called his disciples. The Risen Jesus appears to his disciples on a majestic mountain, the most important setting in Matthew's gospel for teaching and revelation. As did the women, the male disciples respond with reverence when they see Jesus and they worship him (verse 17). Yet some of them also doubt, a word which connotes uncertainty and hesitation at this first encounter with the Risen One. This mixture of adoration and doubt, of faith and indecision, is characteristic of Christian discipleship until the close of the age.

The Risen Jesus proclaims the universality of the authority bestowed upon him by the Father. The declaration echoes the text of Daniel 7:14, concerning the exalted Son of Man: "To him was given dominion and glory and kingship, that all peoples, nations, and languages should serve him. His dominion is an everlasting dominion that shall not pass away, and his kingship is one that shall never be destroyed." The glory of Jesus seen by the disciples at the transfiguration becomes the permanent mode of his life as the risen and exalted Lord. His manifestation on the mountain indicates that the final age is upon the earth and is an anticipation of his final coming in glory.

The universal lordship of Jesus means a universal mission for his church. In Daniel 7 and in the climax of Matthew's gospel, the authority of the Son of Man is given over to his community (Dan 7:18, 22, 27). Because the authority of Jesus has been made universal by his resurrection, Jesus directs his church to a worldwide mission (verse 19). The mission of the disciples, previously restricted by Jesus to proclaiming the kingdom to the people of Israel alone, is now directed to all people, Jews and Gentiles. Jesus commissions them to "go" to the nations. The people of the world will not come unless the disciples go to them.

The central responsibility of the disciples is to make more disciples. The commissioning reflects the threefold mission of the church: evangelization, baptism, and teaching. The initial task is the proclamation of the good news. Then new disciples are brought into the life of the church through baptism. Finally, detailed teaching in the way of Christ must form and guide new disciples.

This entire mission of the church is possible only because of the promise of the risen Lord: "I am with you always, to the end of the age" (verse 20). Though the responsibilities of disciples are daunting, the resources that are available to them in Jesus' authority and presence are more than adequate for the task. The disciples will experience his abiding presence in his church, through the same Spirit that empowered Jesus during his public life. The presence of Jesus will give confidence to disciples in every age, guiding and confirming their decisions, as they await his coming again. Then he will reign over all humanity and all creation as the glorious King.

## Reflection and Discussion

• Though many explanations have been put forward to refute the resurrection, the witness of the church continues to proclaim, "He has been raised." What are the most important indications of the truth of the resurrection?

• What is the threefold task that Jesus gave to his disciples? In what ways does the church continue this mission today?

• In what ways does Jesus remain with his church today? In what particular ways do I experience his presence?

• What are some of the truths about Jesus that Matthew has highlighted in his gospel? What is the primary message I want to remember?

## Prayer

*Universal Lord, all authority in heaven and on earth has been given to you by the Father. Give me the desire to worship you and the courage to be a witness to your resurrection. Help me to do your will on earth as it is in heaven until you come in glory.*

# SUGGESTIONS FOR FACILITATORS, GROUP SESSION 6

1. Welcome group members and make any final announcements or requests.

2. You may want to pray this prayer as a group:

*God of all the nations, you have redeemed the world through the crucifixion and death of your Son, and you have renewed creation through his rising to new life. Give us the grace to open our hearts to the love manifested on the cross and the hope revealed through the resurrection. May we be disciples who both gather to worship you and go out to witness to the gospel of salvation. Help us work together to build your church on earth and welcome others into the life of your kingdom. May we always give you glory and honor, through your Son Jesus Christ, in the unity of the Holy Spirit.*

3. Ask one or more of the following questions:
   • How has this study of Matthew's gospel enriched your life?
   • In what way has this study challenged you the most?

4. Discuss lessons 25 through 30. Choose one or more of the questions for reflection and discussion from each lesson to discuss as a group.

5. Ask the group if they would like to study another in the Threshold Bible Study series. Discuss the topic and dates, and make a decision among those interested. Ask the group members to suggest people they would like to invite to participate in the next study series.

6. Ask the group to discuss the insights that stand out most from this study over the past six weeks.

7. Conclude by praying aloud the following prayer or another of your own choosing:

*Holy Spirit of the living God, you inspired the writers of Scripture and you have guided our study during these weeks. Continue to deepen our love for the word of God in the holy gospels and draw us more deeply into the heart of Jesus. We thank you for the confident hope you have placed within us and the gifts which build up the church. Through this study, lead us to worship and witness more fully and fervently, and bless us now and always with the fire of your love.*

# THE **GOSPEL OF MATTHEW** IN THE SUNDAY LECTIONARY

KEY: **Reading** Sunday or feast *(Lectionary #-Cycle)*

**Matthew 1:1–25**
Christmas: Vigil Mass
*(13-ABC)*

**Matthew 1:18–24**
4th Sunday of Advent *(10-A)*

**Matthew 2:1–12**
The Epiphany of the Lord
*(20-ABC)*

**Matthew 2:13–15, 19–23**
Sunday in Octave of
Christmas: Holy Family *(17-A)*

**Matthew 3:1–12**
2nd Sunday of Advent *(4-A)*

**Matthew 3:13–17**
Sunday after Epiphany:
Baptism of the Lord *(21-A)*

**Matthew 4:1–11**
1st Sunday of Lent *(22-A)*

**Matthew 4:12–23**
3rd Sunday in OT *(67-A)*

**Matthew 5:1–12a**
4th Sunday in OT *(70-A)*

**Matthew 5:13–16**
5th Sunday in OT *(73-A)*

**Matthew 5:17–37**
6th Sunday in OT *(76-A)*

**Matthew 5:38–48**
7th Sunday in OT *(79-A)*

**Matthew 6:24–34**
8th Sunday in OT *(82-A)*

**Matthew 7:21–27**
9th Sunday in OT *(85-A)*

**Matthew 9:9–13**
10th Sunday in OT *(88-A)*

**Matthew 9:36—10:8**
11th Sunday in OT *(91-A)*

**Matthew 10:26–33**
12th Sunday in OT *(94-A)*

**Matthew 10:37–42**
13th Sunday in OT *(97-A)*

**Matthew 11:2–11**
3rd Sunday of Advent *(7-A)*

**Matthew 11:25–30**
14th Sunday in OT *(100-A)*

**Matthew 13:1–23**
15th Sunday in OT *(103-A)*

**Matthew 13:24–43**
16th Sunday in OT *(106-A)*

**Matthew 13:44–52**
17th Sunday in OT *(109-A)*

**Matthew 14:13–21**
18th Sunday in OT *(112-A)*

**Matthew 14:22–33**
19th Sunday in OT *(115-A)*

**Matthew 15:21–28**
20th Sunday in OT *(118-A)*

**Matthew 16:13–20**
21st Sunday in OT *(121-A)*

**Matthew 16:21–27**
22nd Sunday in OT *(124-A)*

**Matthew 17:1–9**
2nd Sunday of Lent *(25-A)*

**Matthew 18:15–20**
23rd Sunday in OT *(127-A)*

**Matthew 18:21–35**
24th Sunday in OT *(130-A)*

**Matthew 20:1–16a**
25th Sunday in OT *(133-A)*

**Matthew 21:1–11**
Palm Sunday:
Procession of Palms *(37-A)*

**Matthew 21:28–32**
26th Sunday in OT *(136-A)*

**Matthew 21:33–43**
27th Sunday in OT *(139-A)*

**Matthew 22:1–14**
28th Sunday in OT *(142-A)*

**Matthew 22:15–21**
29th Sunday in OT *(145-A)*

**Matthew 22:34–40**
30th Sunday in OT *(148-A)*

**Matthew 23:1–12**
31st Sunday in OT *(151-A)*

**Matthew 24:37–44**
1st Sunday of Advent *(1-A)*

**Matthew 25:1–13**
32nd Sunday in OT *(154-A)*

**Matthew 25:14–30**
33rd Sunday in OT *(157-A)*

**Matthew 25:31–46**
34th Sunday in OT:
Christ the King *(160-A)*

**Matthew 26:14—27:66**
Palm Sunday of the
Lord's Passion *(38-A)*

**Matthew 28:1–10**
Easter Vigil *(41-A)*

**Matthew 28:16–20**
Ascension of the Lord *(58-A)*

**Matthew 28:16–20**
Sunday after Pentecost:
Holy Trinity (165-B)